LOWCOUNTRY VOODOO

A TO Z

CAROLE MARSH LONGMEYER

D0920310

Copyright Copyright 2016 Carole Marsh Longmeyer
All rights reserved.

Printed in the United States of America.

Published by Gallopade International, Peachtree City, Georgia.

For permissions or author interview, contact Gallopade at 800-536-2438.

Lowcountry Voodoo Team:

Susan Van Denhende, Graphic design and illustrations
Jon McKenna, Gallopade New Product Development
Janice Baker and Kathy Dean, editors
John Hanson, Art Director
Tommy Dean, Printing and Binding

Note: There are many mentions of herbs and such, and what they may or may not cure; remember this is folklore and never use something you have no explicit medical knowledge or approval of, please. Also, although there are references to online sources of such items, neither the author nor the publisher endorse such purchases unless you are familiar with the source and how to tell if you are getting the real deal or not. This book is merely to share history, reference, facts, legend, lore, and more: we neither endorse any person, place or item in this book, living, dead, or something in between. Just remember, while some things may be true, poison is still poison. Enjoy, but use common sense, please.

Also by Carole Marsh Longmeyer

SLIGHTLY SOUTH OF HEAVEN
Sensational and Unsavory Crimes in the Lowcountry

DEATH BY GRITS
Surprising Tales of Murder by Food, Often at the Hands of Your Favorite Person

THE KUDZU COOKBOOK
Cooking Up a Storm with that Wild & Crazy Vine that Grows in Miles-Per-Hour!

Dedicated to those who believe the unbelievable, love the unloved, wash the unwashed; you are special.

Hoodoo you do?

Roots, hexes and spells
Asphidity bags;
Dr. Buzzard and haint blue,
And riding boo-hags.

Long live this lore
That came to our shore,
And seems destined to haunt us
Forevermore.

Overturned Tombstones

Overturned tombstones
Mark the place
Where restless ghosts
Begin to pace.

Who can blame them
Covered with sand,
To wish again
To roam the land

Of beginnings
That they made,
Only now
To haunt a grave.

—Carole Marsh Longmeyer

Table of Contents

Getting to the Root of the Matter 15
Note on References 21
A-Z 22
Bibliography 166
Resources 172
Acknowledgements 175
About the Author 178
About the Designer & Illustrator 178

LOWCOUNTRY VOODOO A TO Z

Carole Marsh Longmeyer
Illustrated by Susan Van Denhende

Getting to the Root of the Matter...

My introduction to voodooish stuff came via my grandmother, Mama Byrd. She was a big believer in signs, potions, spells and such. She was not Gullah; she was not Geechee. She couldn't have pointed out Haiti on a map. I'm not even sure where her interest or instinctual affinity for such things came from, but it was visceral and omnipresent.

When my sister, Suzanne, and I would sashay down Peachtree Street in downtown Atlanta on the way to our grandmother's three a.m. to three p.m. shift as a switchboard operator at the famed Dinkler Hotel, we had no fear. In the palm of her hand, Mama Byrd carried a large two-sided (taped on one edge) razor blade. If we passed anyone who even gave us a "look," she'd brandish her weapon at the possible accoster and squeal: "I'll cut you all to pieces!" Invariably, they skittered away into the darkness. She was her own one-woman witchdoctress!

Before we left Mama Byrd's apartment, my sister and I were charged with sprinkling fine baby powder at the doorway threshold, the better to know when someone had snuck inside and left illicit tell-tale footprints. We also had to pluck (painfully) strands of hair for her to lick and stick across the doorjamb, also as evidence, if broken upon our return, of a trespasser.

It all seemed great fun. Not so much fun was the night when we were all sleeping in her big, four-poster bed and I awoke and swore that there was a man standing in the corner. She pulled out her pistol…and shot that shadow dead! Mama Byrd was a strong spirit.

Mustard plasters were her cure for croup; whiskey, honey and lemon the (much better) cure for cough.

The asphidity bag around her neck was always a conundrum to us. A leather pouch about the size of a walnut, we would spy her

stuffing it with secret ingredients, presumably medicinal herbs and roots. But to my sister and I, they were magic potions, and probably, knowing our grandmother, black magic.
As a seamstress, she had an abundant supply of very long pins, with which to poke and prod fabric effigies of those she felt needed reprimanding. She never used the term "voodoo doll," but we knew what Mama Byrd was up to.

Midnight rollercoaster rides across the north Georgia mountains to Chattanooga, Tennessee were necessitated by a sudden extreme urgency to visit the fortune teller. Even as a young teen, I was always suspicious of the apparently rich, tall, thin, pale man in the house cantilevered over the mountain's edge. Hard-earned dollars passed into his skeletal hands. I was never privy to what happened next, but I hoped the money bought us safely back down the steep, two-lane road, chased in the rainstorm by speeding eighteen-wheelers, brakes screeching as Mama Byrd slowed and swerved to take in the view.

Although I never experienced it, my sister was with my mother and grandmother on more than one occasion when an eerie blue light would suddenly fill the car. It was not a scary entity, but highly visible and present, its nature, meaning and intent unknown, though my mother insisted it gave her a peaceful feeling.

As an unwilling possessor of ESP (extra sensory perception) as a child, teen and young adult, I had no reason to doubt such woo-woo things, having experienced them to a powerful, and equally inexplicable, degree many times. On any given day, I might keel over with a stabbing pain in my chest and later learn that a close relative had had a heart attack at that exact moment. These unbidden and inexplicable events happened to me many times over the years.

I spent a lot of time in Savannah as a kid. It all seemed a web of magic and spells, hoodoo and voodoo—long before John Berendt's blockbuster book *Midnight in the Garden of Good and Evil.* Later, as a researcher and writer, my bent was toward mysteries and the mysterious. The more I read and learned and witnessed, I became a believer, not in hokey television and movie voodoo, but in the real thing.

What is the real thing? I actually think it rests with the Gullah-Geechee, as well as in the Lowcountry of Louisiana, of course. Those who came to the shores of early America, against their will, brought nothing to sustain them but the ancient culture and beliefs of their ancestors. I believe it's a wide, gray swath, much like the swash line of the sea that represents the spectrum of spells and potions and such. After all, don't we all want something to grasp onto in times of trouble, to foil evil, to enhance our lives and control our future and our fate? If you just guffawed, tell me you never sought out a four-leaf clover, hung your keys on a rabbit's foot, made a wish on a shooting star, tossed salt over your shoulder, or bought a lottery ticket.

Hoodoo you do? I love this Lowcountry legend and lore, well knowing that the truth is often much stranger than any fiction we can imagine. Having said that, enjoy this A-to-Z exploration of all things voodoo, at least here in the Lowcountry. Perhaps then you can explore what such things might still ride the night wind (and even bare necks) in your neck of the woods. I'll just bet they do!

Carole Marsh Longmeyer
Palmetto Bluff, at the tri-crossroads of the May River, mayhem and magic—a beautiful place to be!

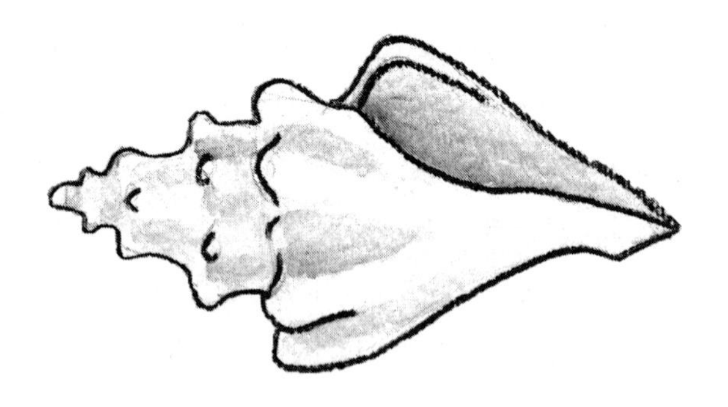

Note on References

There has been a lot written on voodoo/hoodoo over the years. I tried to pick the best research available. Of special note [see bibliography]:

Coffin Point: The Strange Cases of Ed McTeer, WitchDoctor Sheriff by Baynard Woods—A great new, short book on Beaufort County, SC's famous witchdoctor sheriff, Ed McTeer, and his relationship with the infamous Dr. Buzzard; rumors are a movie or television series might be in the making.

Hoodoo Herb and Root Magic by Catherine Yronwode—A wealth of information on the use of roots, herbs, minerals, zoological curios and other hoodoo doodahs; includes interesting actual botanical uses as well.

The Mind Game by E. Fuller Torrey—A fascinating older book on the kindred spirits: witchdoctors and psychiatrists.

The Serpent and the Rainbow by Wade Davis—A Harvard scientist's exploration of Haitian voodoo; rather astonishing.

Alligator tooth: Lordy, we have these aplenty in the Lowcountry. A gator tooth is the Southern equivalent of a lucky badger tooth in other parts of the country. You can carry the tooth in a pocket and "feed" it with whiskey, urine, or other conjure concoctions to enhance its power. Alligator teeth are said to be powerful mojos for all kinds of gambling, including bingo and the lottery. Since gators naturally shed their teeth, they are fairly plentiful. An alligator foot is another type of conjure curio, although just how you put your hands on one, I would not want to speculate. It's also called a gator paw.

Altar: A place set up to perform rituals, use charms, and place your voodoo dolls.

Amulet: An ornament or small piece of jewelry worn to provide protection from disease, evil, or other bad things.

Animal names: Most root doctors take on animal names, thus Dr. Buzzard, Dr. Bug, Dr. Crow, Dr. Fly, Dr. Snake, Dr. Turtle, etc. I'm still searching for a Dr. Gopher Tortoise…or a Dr. Shark.

Ankle bracelet: To ward off evil, wear an ankle bracelet made of dimes soaked in the entrails of a live frog.

Anointing oil: Use on the outer edge of your gris-gris or mojo bag to ensure a charm works. Use love oil, protection oil, etc., depending on what you want to achieve. It is believed that certain scents have a powerful effect on people. Wear a love potion, for example, if you are eager for a certain person to fall in love with you. As for myself, I wear Birthday Cake perfume; it works really well to gain the love of old men, as well as the adoration of little children.

Apothecaries: Early drug stores or pharmacies in America often sold voodoo items such as love potions, sprinkling powders, herbs, and such. Today Internet websites are awash in voodoo websites selling conjuring doodahs of all types.

Asafoetida: A stinky herb often called Devil's Dung, its use dates back to magical traditions in Europe and India. The herb is useful for all sorts of conjure, including (but not limited to) preventing disease, keeping away the law, stopping someone from pestering you, revenge, reversing a trick and jinxing an enemy. My grandmother once wore an asafoetida bag around her neck, but I believe she filled it with Chanel No. 5.

Auto-suggestion: Some people suggest that a belief in voodoo is self-induced; if you believe, it is true, or comes true. There have been instances of impotence and even suicide brought on by intense belief in apparent voodoo happenings. If you do not believe this is possible, perhaps you have not read enough well-documented instances of such things.

Bad luck: There is no end to unlucky omens in the land of Lowcountry voodoo! Just a few bad luck signs include: never try on someone's hat…never let anyone comb your hair…don't stomp your left foot…leave a tail's-up coin alone…if you stub your toe, be sure to turn around in a circle…don't look in a mirror with someone else…never walk backwards…don't keep a crowing hen…never bring a spade or hoe into the house…never lend matches… don't dream of chickens…don't sleep with your hands clasped behind your head…never mend clothes being worn at the time...and, the usual "if a black cat crosses in front of you…" and "if you break a mirror…". As the song says, "If I didn't have bad luck, I'd have no luck at all!"

Bad roots: Animal parts, like crow feathers, salamander feet, or a black cat's left thigh bone (preferably from a cat that has been burned alive).

Baptisms: Many slaves were eager to be baptized, even if they stuck to their old native ways of worship, as well. They insisted on being baptized in their local waters on a falling tide so the river would carry their sins out to sea.

Bats: Not surprisingly, dried bat, bat wings, bat hearts, and bat blood are much-desired items for conjuring. Bats are endangered enough as it is, without being in great demand for charms and such. Fortunately, since the 1920s, Bat's Blood Ink (once the real thing) is now just red ink with added scents, used for writing pacts. I think my lawyer has a bottle.

Beans and Peas: Probably no other thing is more common in conjure than these legumes. Around the world, there are endless conjurable peas and beans suitable for amulets, casting spells, lucky charms, and eating, such as black-eyed peas at New Year's for luck throughout the coming year.

Better than a Scarecrow

In the old days, Gullah farmers came up with an ingenious way to protect their crops from hungry deer. They would dig a small pond by a field. Next they would catch an alligator and move it into the pond. The gator would observe the deer roaming through the crop rows and soon learned that they were easy pickings!

Big Dig

In the 1950s, a St. Helena Island man suffered illness and money problems; he sincerely believed that some enemy of his had buried an evil root in his yard, which as he walked over it daily, was causing all his problems. Instead of consulting a root doctor, he proceeded to dig up his yard, one shovelful of dirt at a time. He never found the root and died soon after. His daughter, convinced that the root remained, and fearful of the troubles it would cause her, set their house afire and burned it to the ground.

Black Cat Bone: Animal shelters are rightly suspicious when someone wants to adopt an all-black cat. While we can hope this seldom happens, the black cat bone charm is obtained thus: toss the cat alive into a cauldron of boiling water at midnight (in a graveyard or at a crossroads)...boil until meat falls off the bone...search for the cat's magical bone, i.e., the one that can give you the power of invisibility. Fortunately, it has been proven that black cat bone sold online is generally a piece of chicken bone painted black.

Black Cat Dust: This is made with the powdered left front shoulder bone of a black cat, mixed with a ground up lodestone. Supposedly, it attracts good luck. I once found a perfectly flat dead black cat in the basement of a house I bought, but it did not occur to me (at all!) that it might be potential good luck; nor did I have the urge or instinct to grind it up.

Black Cow's Milk: The South is a land of dairies. Black cows are especially prized. The use for black cow's milk in conjure is myriad—a cure for: a lightning strike; smoke inhalation; snakebite; shingles; 'live things in you.' "Mix the milk with lard and grease your rectum" is the specific advice, FYI.

Black Magic: (Also called dark magic.) Traditionally refers to the use of supernatural powers or magic for selfish or evil purposes.

Blessing: A type of spell or prayer to spiritually cleanse a person, place, or thing with positive energy and one's hopes.

Blue Root: A particularly feared root said to cause wells to dry up, cows to cease giving milk, hens to stop laying eggs, physical ailments, mental illness, and even death.

Blue sunglasses: Want to spy a genuine root doctor? Look for someone wearing blue-lens sunglasses; I have a pair myself, but only because I like the sky to still look blue on a cloudy day.

Blueing: Bluestone is often used as an ingredient in mojo hands made by hoodoo doctors; it can bring gamblers' luck or protection from evil. An early floor wash was used to keep away evil spirits. Also called blue vitriol or blue copperas, it's actually copper sulphate. This substance is haint blue in color, and deadly since it's highly toxic. Therefore, witchdoctors use ordinary laundry blueing in their rootwork.

Bo' Hog Root: In the Lowcountry, lovage root is known by this name and carried in a red flannel bag to attract a new lover.

Boo-daddy: This charm protects you from a bugaloo. It must be made by a conjurer with plough mud, moss, sweetgrass, and saltwater placed inside an amulet or charm bag and worn on your person for protection.

Boo hag: A bad spirit, a boo hag uses witchcraft to get a person to do what they want. At night, a boo hag can shed her skin and become invisible. This spirit can "ride" a person by sitting on his or her chest. You will know this from the pressure and the smell of rotting meat. You can sometimes foil a boo hag by putting a broom by your door; she will stop to count the straws, which may take her until dawn, when her powers cease and she has to don her skin once more. (Brushes, sieves, and strainers also work.) It's also helpful to paint your doors and window shutters haint blue, and to scatter salt around and burn candles throughout the night.

Boogers: (S'not the nose kind!) If you see a "booger," it may appear as an alligator, but have four legs on each side. This creature can have large, coal red eyes, breath smoke, and otherwise scare the bejesus out of you. It is advised to recite the Lord's Prayer to scare the booger away. Wish I had known that when I'd head to Callawassie Island's pool to swim at night. By the time many "boogers" had crossed the road in my headlights, I had tucked-tail and headed back home—"high and dry and all my fingers and toes" is my motto!

Botanica: A retail or online store that sells spiritual goods such as herbs, oils, and other natural items.

Bottle tree: You'll see these around the Lowcountry… small, strong-limbed bushes or trees with upside down cobalt blue bottles stuck on various limbs. This is so any bad spirits can go up into the bottles, but not escape. I want one to see if it also works for mosquitoes.

Broom: The Lowcountry is a land of grasses and broom of all types. "Broom" may imply broom corn (sorghum), Scotch broom or Pampas grass. Sweetgrass is harvested and woven into highly-prized (and priced) baskets. In conjure, brooms and broom straw are used to cleanse, purify and protect. While witches ride brooms, broom straws or brooms, strategically situated, can ward off witches and other unwelcome visitors.

Bugaloo: This big, bad daddy comes out of the deep woods on moonless nights to take retribution for perceived or actual wrongs. (It is not a dance; the only dance is you running for your life!)

Bull of the Woods: A tea that is said to make you vomit grass.

Butting: To cut off the tip of a candle, turn it upside down, and dig a new tip out of the bottom, as a way to reverse people or conditions; also called flipping.

Buzzard cures: This dirty bird is good for many a voodoo thing. Make a stinky salve to stop muscle pain. Burn feathers and mix with vinegar to make a paste to plaster on a door to keep evil away. Steal a buzzard egg and boil it; remove the embryo and replace the egg. Wait for the buzzard to crack open the egg with a stone. What you want is the stone. This hard-won talisman is said to have great power to protect you from all evil. Note: In Charleston and New Orleans in the 1930s, burglars believed such stones (or shells, whichever was used) made them invisible in the dark.

Buzzy: Nickname of Dr. Buzzard's son-in-law, who received the mantle to practice conjuring after the doctor's death at Oaks Plantation on St. Helena Island.

Casting a spell: Let's conjure, ya'll! Black magic can be made with charms or voodoo dolls, but neither will be effective unless you perform some kind of ritual first. [Also see Black Magic, Charms and Voodoo Dolls.]

Catnip: Not only is this beloved by cats and a common herbal treatment for children's colic, in conjure, it's also a love herb believed to make women enticing and charming to men.

Cat's Eye Shell: Fortunately (for cats), this does not come from a cat. It is the operculum shell of the turbo, an ocean-dwelling herbivorous mollusk. In conjure it is known as a protective curio, which can ward off Evil Eye. Amulets were made from such shells and worn around the neck for protection. I find exceedingly charming the variety of ways so many conjure items can be used.

For example, to protect from slander (to be specific), you should carry your cat's eye shell in a red flannel bag with rue and slippery elm for (and I quote from *Hoodoo Herb and Root Magic*) "immunity from harmful tales told by covetous neighbors, back-biters on the job, and hidden enemies posing as friends." I am headed to the beach!

Celery: This vegetable is commonly used in conjuring to enhance psychic powers. You might burn celery seed on charcoal to create incense, or brew tea from crushed seeds. I still just serve mine the old-fashioned way with pimento cheese.

Chanting: When you are trying to charm, chant in a soft voice, not high-pitched or loud.

Charmed, I'm Sure-I

The vast array of spiritual, divinatory, cleansing, lucky, and other spells runs the gamut of needs; choose wisely.

Achieve marital fidelity
Achieve success
Attract luck
Attract money
Bar people
Beauty
Bind enemies
Break jinxes
Break up a romance
Break up old conditions
Cast off bad habits
Catch adulterers
Change luck
Cleanse and purify
Command respect
Confuse opponents
Contact the dead
Control dogs
Control or dominate
Converse with spirits
Courage, bravery
Cure venomous snake bites
Divine
Dream lucky dreams
Family blessings
Favors
Fertility, childbirth
Find a murderer

Find hidden treasure
Friendship
Gain musical skills
Gain power
Gain wisdom and insight
Gambling luck
Get a job, promotion or raise
Get bank loans
Get eloquence
Get revenge
Health
Hot foot it; get away
Increase lactation
Invisibility
Jinx someone
Keep away unwanted visitors
Keep the law away
Long life
Make voodoo dolls
Mental health
Painless baby teething
Peace at home
Prevent accidents
Prevent hag-riding
Prevent theft
Protect from lightning
Protect from snakes
Protect your home

Protect yourself
Put live things in someone
Receive blessings
Receive omens
Reconcile with a lover
Remove sin
Rent out rooms, property
Repel evil
Repel jinxes
Resolve legal matters
Restore sexuality
Return tricks
Reverse evil
Safe travel
Shield from unnatural illnesses
Sound sleep
Stop gossip
Stop marital infidelity
Stop nightmares
Stop witchcraft
Strength
Summon spirits
Take live things out of you
Ward off evil eye
Warn of evil
Write pacts
-just to name a few!

Charmed, I'm Sure-II

There are as many charms as you can imagine. Here's a list of some of the most charming ones I found:

Attraction Charm
Breakup Charm
Cast Off Evil Charm
Fast Luck Charm
Hot Foot Charm
Kiss Me Charm
Law Keep Away Charm
Money Charm
Peaceful Home Charm
Psychic Vision Charm
Real Estate Charm
Reconciliation Charm
Stay With Me Charm
Steady Work Charm
Stop Gambling Charm
Uncrossing Charm
Wisdom Charm

Charms: There are many different names for voodoo charms: gris-gris bags, conjure bags, ouanga bags, mojo bags. These small leather or cloth bags may be filled with roots, herbs, powders, stones, feathers, bones, cloth, hair, fingernails, used tissues, four-leaf clovers, a rabbit's foot, dice, talismans, patron saint medals, coins, a crucifix, and most anything else.

Meanings of charms:

Coins=wealth
Crucifix=faith
Dice=wealth; good luck
Four-leaf clover=good luck
Patron saint medals=protection
Rabbit's foot=good luck
Talisman=protection

Cocoa: Medically, cocoa is a brain stimulant, diuretic, and vasodilator. In conjure, cocoa beans can be put in a muslin bag and steeped in bathwater. Those who hoodoo swear this wards off depression, improves concentration, and increases emotional well-being.

Coffin Point: An island plantation in Beaufort County, South Carolina; once home to Ed McTeer, sheriff and professed black magic practitioner. In my experience, folks from Coffin Point (and St. Helena Island) take great pride in their origins. Dr. Buzzard lived at Coffin Point. It seems well-named and well-appointed as some unofficial ground zero for hoodoo. I visit, just not after dark.

Cold Reading: A technique used by disreputable fortune-tellers, psychics, and mediums; hot reading is the real psychic deal.

Collards: There's nothing prettier in the Lowcountry fall than a garden of collards gleaming in the sun, and nothing tastier than a mess of collards after the first frost, cooked and served with cornpone. Collards are eaten with black-eyed peas on New Year's Day for good luck in the coming year. Br'er Rabbit kept a pinch of collard seeds, a piece of calmus root, and a rabbit foot in a tasseled money purse for good luck. This was known as Br'er Rabbit's Money Mojo.

Conditioning Oil: Oils that have a specific use in a spell, such as Cast Off Evil Oil, Follow Me Boy or Money Drawing Oil.

Conjure: To make magic. A Gullah conjurer performs black magic; a root doctor (or witchdoctor), white magic.

Conjure Cook-Off: Sponsored annually in Forestville, California by the Ladies Auxiliary of Missionary Independent Spiritual Church. Voodoo vegetarian recipes welcome—love cookies, etc.

Conjure horses: Said to be common after the Civil War, these creatures appeared larger than normal, breathed fire, and followed nighttime travelers for miles, generally at treetop height. They roared.

Coosaw Island, SC: After a man murdered his wife, he was supposedly lured to Lucy Point Creek by a plateye spirit in the form of his dead wife. He met his demise there.

Cooter: Cooters are aquatic, flat-shelled river turtles, also known as Southern terrapins. Their name comes from the African word kouta, which means terrapin. They grow to 15-17 inches across and can live 40 years. In cooter conjuring, the creatures are never destroyed (although, alas, today, habitat destruction is reducing their numbers). One way to conjure with a cooter is to write the name of a person on its back, set it free in the river, and when it leaves, so will the person. This is commonly known as the To Make Your Lover's Other Partner Move Away conjure.

Crossroads: Places of great spiritual power where magical items are often disposed of and rituals performed, or pacts signed.

Crossroads University: *"Passing down the root, one course at the time"* is their slogan. The school's goal is to share the ancient wisdom of conjuring and related cultural traditions, especially from the American South. In addition to regular coursework, students are required (at their own cost) to acquire 120 hours of practical experience with an authentic witchdoctor in order to receive a Certification in Professional Rootwork. (Note: that would be CPR.) The school also sponsors an annual Hoodoo Almanac, Conjure Library, Conjure Club, and is affiliated with the American Rootwork Association. It's worth visiting their rather lovely website just to see the photographs of the faculty. Also note: a misspelling elsewhere referred to this online school as *Crosstoads* University, which I found much more illustrative of their offerings!

Cures: Just a few examples: Put a potato in your pocket to cure rheumatism. Poke a hole in a dime and tie it around your ankle for general good health. Tie a string around your head to cure headache. To prevent swimmer's cramps, tie a piece of cotton around your ankle.

Cures and Conjuring

So many charms, spells, and other hoodoo/ voodoo hark back to natural herbs and roots and their original medicinal uses. Here are just a few of the common herbs and other botanicals used as natural cures, as well as in conjure.

Adam and Eve plant: *Apelectrum hyemale;* said to be able to calm a restless heart or cure a heartache.

Alligator root: Used as a sedative.

Basil leaves: Put in your bath as a natural deodorant.

Bitterweed: May cure the chills.

Blackroot: Can enforce projectile vomiting as needed in case of poisoning.

Bloodroot tea: Used on skin rashes.

Brambleberry: Mix ashes from the burned sticks with bluestone and alum; chew well and spit on your sores.

Bull nettle: *Solanum carolense;* reputed cure for epilepsy.

Cassena: This holly-like shrub, common in Lowcountry sea islands, contains a powerful stimulant, used instead of coffee or tea.

Chamomile tea: Once, people added a little honey to put any sweet, but colicky, baby to sleep. Today, with allergies, not so much!

Cockroach tea: May help stop persistent cough. (May stop me from ever drinking tea again!)

Dog fennel root tea: Used to invigorate oneself.

Dogwood root, cherry root and oak bark tea: Used to reduce muscular swelling.

Earthworm tea: Mixed with lard and used as a salve for rashes.

Ginger root tea: Used for irregular or stopped menses.

Green cocklebururs: Used as a poultice for skin ailments.

Gunpowder and whiskey: Whisk together to calm your heart and give you power.

Heartleaf plant: Make a wash to clear bloodshot eyes and blurred vision.

Peppermint oil: Used to settle troubled stomachs.

Persimmon, sapwood and maple bark tea: Used to calm cataracts.

Psylicibe cubensis: A blue-white mushroom that grows naturally in manure from Gullah cows and ponies.

Sassafras tea: Boiled from the roots of the Life Everlasting plant, it was used as a tonic and cold remedy.

Smokeless gunpowder: Contains nitroglycerin, a heart stimulant.

Turpentine: Gullah have used it as an emergency balm, antibiotic, and seal for cuts, especially back when they worked in the piney woods on naval stores, such as turpentine, pitch and tar.

Wild grapevine sap: Diluted, it may help with incontinence.

Curse: A type of spell used to bring harm to a person in order to punish them, teach them a lesson, or some related goal.

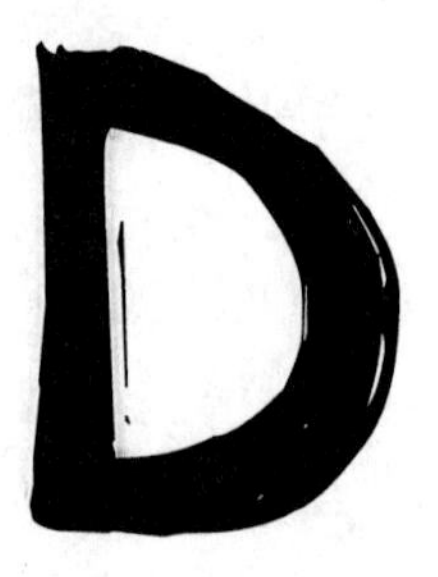

"Daddy Snakelegs" Alexander: From Richmond, Virginia; famous for using Colubrid Blacksnakes in his conjures. He'd kill them and hang them upside down to drain their blood, which he preserved in whiskey to dose drinks to produce "Live Things in You." He would then take the dried snake body and powder it to make goofer dust for his clients.

Days of the Week

Remember the old Monday, Tuesday, etc. panties? Well, days of the week figure strongly in voodoo rituals. Each day is said to be ruled by a different planet and has a particular astrological meaning:

Sunday...the Sun...yellow...peace and harmony; so a good day to perform a ritual about friendship.

Monday...the Moon...white...love and fertility; a powerful day for love charms.

Tuesday...Mars...red; the day to break curses, challenge enemies.

Wednesday...Mercury...purple; cast spells of good health.

Thursday...Jupiter...blue; it's time to focus on wealth, luck and ambition.

Friday...Venus...green; rituals might focus on happiness, love and romance.

Saturday...Saturn...black; your choices are conjuring evil or protecting yourself from evil.

Death: Gullah people believe that your soul leaves the body when you die and returns to God. However, your spirit remains on Earth to intercede as necessary with loved ones left behind. Spirits can be good or bad, protective or tormenting. To keep the dead from returning to haunt you, respectful funerals include passing children over the grave, prized possessions left to appease the dead, and broken dishes to indicate that the "chain" of death has been broken.

Death by Voodoo: Many Gullah beliefs relate to death and dying. For example: Turn mirrors to the wall so the corpse won't be reflected. Allow ancestors to enter the graveyard before you do. Stop any clock in the home at the time of death. Don't sweep until the dead person has been removed from the home. If you hear a rooster crow in the night, someone will be dead by dawn. A howling dog means someone is dying.

Death Touch: Someone who is deemed to be able to cause death through touching a person or object that the person then touches.

'de patch': Local Lowcountry truck farms that grow cucumbers, tomatoes, melons, and other crops that thrive in the sandy, coastal soil.

Disney: A voodoo doll appeared in the 2009 animated Disney movie, *The Princess and the Frog*.

Divination: The ritual process of gaining information about the past, present, or future, using tools such as Tarot Cards, psychic powers, or observation of signs or omens.

Doctrine of Signatures: This concept specifies that how a plant looks indicates how it should be used.

Dr. Buzzard

His real name was Stephaney Robinson. Beginning in the early 1900s, he served as the local root doctor on St. Helena Island in South Carolina. The tiny crossroads of Frogmore was his base. But Dr. Buzzard was not just a local entity; he sold his roots to thousands of eager followers nationwide. Among his many purported skills was the ability to pick winning lottery numbers, command spirited haunts and hags in the vicinity, and to put evil roots on a man so powerful that the poor soul was "as good as dead." Dr. Buzzard drove a shiny black Lincoln and dressed impeccably. His uncanny ability to work roots, hexes and spells to achieve goals was revered by many, and many paid dearly for his services. Weekly, he would arrive at Frogmore, site of the St. Helena Island post office, where he retrieved piles of envelopes filled with cash, which he stuffed in his suit pockets. When he opened a letter and found a money order, he tore it up and discarded it, leaving no trace of incriminating evidence that could get him into any legal entanglements.

It was sworn that if you wanted to visit Dr. Buzzard at his Oaks Plantation home, you could just walk down the creek bank and the doctor would send a boat rowed by the wings of two trained buzzards. However, if you were there to trick the doctor, the buzzards would do their best to drown you.

If Dr. Buzzard agreed to help you, it might even be in court at trial. His "speaking in tongues" could pretty much shut up the other lawyers (and everyone else in the courtroom), and yes, he was just as expensive as they were, but for some, a bargain, depending on the results. When he was holding forth, it is said the buzzards that always perched on the Beaufort County water tower would take flight and buzz the courthouse.

When the doctor was suspected in an infamous draft-dodging scheme, he was finally brought to trial. A key witness at first confessed that the root he had obtained from the doctor was supposed to make him invisible. But once in the courtroom, actually facing Dr. Buzzard, the witness had an odd fit of groaning and shaking, beating himself, frothing at the mouth, and such.

Dr. Buzzard continued to foil the law with his intimidating blue sunglasses, and trying to hex courtroom proceedings in his favor. Threatened with contempt of court, a battle ensued between the sheriff and the doctor. After killing a buzzard perched atop the courthouse, Dr. Buzzard's son died in an auto accident. Convinced that the hexer had been out-hexed, the doctor agreed to give up, basically, practicing medicine without a license. Found guilty, he was fined $300. It was no problem for him to pay up, but to accept defeat just took the voodoo wind out of the doctor and he soon died.

Legend has it that, perhaps, Dr. Buzzard was never buried; instead his remains were dismembered and shared with other root workers, so invaluable these icons would have been.

Dr. Spirit: Root doctors have special connections to spirits of all kinds. One of his main requests might be to protect someone from an undesired spirit visitation. Such protection might include special prayers, roots, incense, or powders sprinkled around a doorstep. What a conjureman keepeth away, however, he might also unleash—a further reason to respect your local root doctor, since you never know whose side he's on at the time.

Draft Dodger Conjure

At the start of World War II, like others across the nation, young South Carolina men, black and white, were called up for the draft. So many strapping young African American boys were turned down that it was suspicious. Although the War Department was alerted to the situation, they pretty much ignored it until an entire busload of Gullah draftees arrived singing:

Gonna lay down my sword and shield,
Down by the riverside, down by the riverside,
Gonna lay down my sword and shield,
Down by the riverside,
An' gonna study war no mo'.

It all seemed harmless enough until half the men had to go to the hospital and two died.

Evidence indicated that the men had taken a "potion" of moonshine whiskey and lead arsenate, a lethal combination. The culprit was Dr. Bug, who not only felt the boys should not be forced to go to war if they did not want to, but also that the potion was harmless. He claimed that he drank a shot of it each day himself and would do so now in the courtroom. Found guilty, bond was set. No problem for the doctor. He just called for his "box" and shelled out as many dollars as needed. However, in attendance in the courtroom was the IRS, which further confiscated most of the rest of the box money for unpaid taxes, apparently a new concept for Dr. Bug. Believing he himself had been "rooted," it is said Dr. Bug soon died.

Dream On: Gullah dream signs include wishing on a new moon or dreaming beneath a quilt. If you dream about snakes, you may be facing temptation. Don't give anyone deceased who you dream about what they ask for...only death will follow.

Dressing: In conjure, this is not a sartorial term, but the use of herbs, oils and such applied to other things, ranging from amulets to mojo bags to protective aftershave.

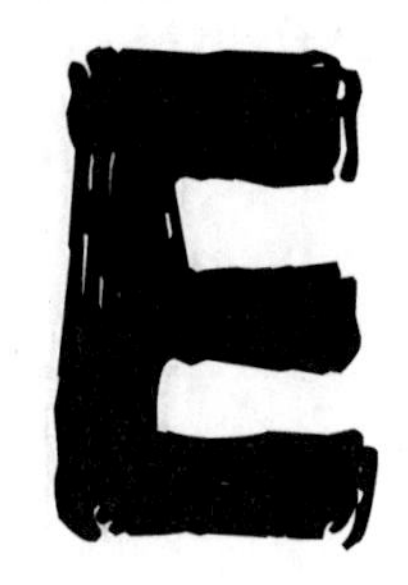

Evil eye: Similar to mouthing. Must be done in person, preferably by a root doctor who casts a spell via looks, signs, speaking in tongues, or other roots.

Evil is as evil does: You can't get rid of evil in the voodoo world. You may exorcise a spirit from a person or a place, but the spirit will find another host or home, and that could be you, or your dwelling, so beware. After all, even the Bible tells of Jesus driving devils from a man into a herd of pigs.

Evil root: If you want to hex a person, it can be done with an 'evil root' buried beneath steps or some other place the person commonly passes over or by.

Faith healers: Herbalists practiced as doctors in plantation slave quarters. Using knowledge of the past paired with newly encountered plants from the fields and swamps, as well as what they learned from local native Indians, they treated their people as best they could. These 'cures' were often more effective than the white doctor's dreaded bloodletting, purges, or plasters. In addition to addressing physical ailments, these herbalists also treated spiritual sicknesses via potions, powders, roots and other methods. Eventually, such healers became known as root doctors.

Fear: A big part of voodoo is fear. If someone were to root me by 'chewing' some unknown evil root, while making signs, speaking in tongues, muttering, swaying, perhaps their eyes rolling back in their head, and juice and spit running down their chin…I'd go running in fear myself!

Feeding: When you 'dress' a mojo bag with oil, or a lodestone with oil or magnetic sand to nourish it and keep it strong to work for you.

Folk magic: Also called black magic. Hoodoo folk magic has its origins in Africa and African American traditions, with a mixture of Native American herbal lore and European folk magic; today, lore from Cuba and Mexico can also be found in hoodoo.

Folk Spells

A less formal form of conjuring, perhaps just a simple ritual with no altar or chanting. Examples include:

You need to defeat an enemy: Write their name on a pink or brown candle; at bedtime, light the candle and state aloud that you are rid of ___________; blow out the candle; repeat each night until the candle is just a nub; bury in your backyard.

You seriously desire a person: Take a mirror this person has gazed into (but that you have not); break it into pieces, put the pieces in a bag and bury them in your backyard. Sprinkle the spot with love herbs. Continue this ritual until the person desires you!

You want to rid yourself of someone: Write the name of the person on a piece of paper an odd number of times (3, 5, 9); put the paper in a jar; fill the jar with vinegar, screw on the lid and toss it into a lake, river or other body of water. Useful to banish a nasty co-worker or other pest in your life.

Follow Me Root: If you have been rooted, this conjuring countermeasure may be effective. Will the rooter then further counter the rootee? Probably. Root doctors count on this temper tantrum tennis match to not only keep the root game going, but also to ratchet up the fees as fast and furious as any legal proceeding imaginable.

Four-leafed clover: While many of us may swear we have nothing to do with superstition, most all of us recall searching for four-leafed clovers for good luck. Long used in European and American history, these charms were often pressed into books or Bibles, flattened in a wallet, or used in jewelry. Supposedly, they bring health, wealth, love, luck, and protect you from witchcraft.

Fraud: Believers in hoodoo and folk magic know that the integrity of an herb, plant, or root is imperative. Once, when a person grew their own plants, they knew the original form of the plant as well as the dried, cut and sifted, boiled, or powdered forms. Because they recognized the leaf, flower, and seeds, they were not misled by false roots. This was of great significance in both herbal medicine and magical herbalism. Today, it is not uncommon to find for sale fake versions of ingredients used in hoodoo, so buyer beware!

Geechee: The name for the Gullah people in Georgia.

Ghost dog: A plateye, or apparition, in the form of a dog that has had an evil spirit enter it. In 1855, a country doctor spotted this "Hound of Goshen"; many other doctors and others swore they had spotted the ghost dog. This dog is quite large, albino, and has a long snout and big tail. It is reported that the dog has been seen as recently as 1998 in the area of Union County, South Carolina.

A Gullah river man refused to guard a loaded barge overnight. When asked if he was afraid of ghosts, the man said, "Ghost ain't gone hurt you. You is gone hurt yo'self gettin' out of the way!"

Ghosts: Also known as "hants" in the Gullah community.

Good luck: While bad luck omens seem to well outnumber good luck ones, grasp onto these Gullah reminders: If you find a coin facing heads-up, toss it over your right shoulder for good luck. Nail a horseshoe over your front door with the ends up so the U can hold in good luck. On the first day of the month, say "Rabbit!" before you get out of bed.

Good Night and Good Luck

- A new mother should sip water from a thimble if she wants her baby to have a painless first tooth.
- A singing bird on a doorstep means company is coming.
- Bubbles in your coffee mean money will come to you.
- Burn a former lover's shoes to have more new lovers.
- Burn your own old shoes and you will never be bitten by a snake.

- Count to nine any time you spy a red bird on your doorstep to receive money.
- Dream beneath a new quilt and your dream will come true.
- Dreams of clear running water mean good luck and money.
- Hang a snake from your porch so your crops will never dry up.
- Hasten childbirth by stuffing your nose with snuff.
- Make a knot of "five finger grass" and hang on your bedpost for a good night's sleep.
- Make a wish to a new moon and it will come true.
- People who wash hands together will be friends forever.
- Pin a snippet of your lover's shirttail to your skirt to keep him faithful.
- Tie a piece of cotton around your ankle to avoid swimmer's cramps.
- To dream of gray horses means you'll have a happy marriage.

Good roots: Herbs, asafoetida, gunpowder, sulphur, salt, red or black candle wax, incense.

Goofer dust: Graveyard dirt gathered just before midnight, right above the corpse's heart. For an evil root, go for a Christian's grave; for a benevolent root, shoot for a criminal's resting spot. It is advised to take care not to disturb the spirits as you harvest this dirt. Leave a new dime on a grave if you don't want to be followed home. Also advisable: prayers, or a good cussin' out. Add sulphur, saltpeter, salt, or sugar to keep the goofer dust active. Other uses for goofer dust include spreading it on your property to keep evil away or inside your shoes so you can walk on evil without picking it up.

Grandma Stories

According to my good friend Laverne, Gullah grandmas are full of voodoo stories to curl your hair, especially if you are a young child eavesdropping. The fascinating thing to me is not the stories, hoodoo-y as they may be, but that they seem to be endless! Here are a few brief ones.

A Leg Up

A woman wrapped her own leg tightly in electrical cords. After this her eyes became wild-looking and devil-red. Apparently, she was rooting another woman who later complained of live things squirming in her legs. After repeated doctor visits, it was finally decided to cut into her leg to discover the source of her problem. When an incision was made—a mess of tiny snakes spewed out!

Flipped Food

To keep her husband, a woman used a traditional voodoo "Keep a Man" conjure. She gathered her own "personal concern" (better known as menstrual blood) and— wait for it: added it to a pot of red rice, which she then served to her man. For as long (years!) as she did this, her man stayed with her and was faithful. However, as soon as she went through menopause, he began to stray and beat her. That this is a common conjure should give men pause!

Fruit of the Loom

The problem with rooting someone is that

it can backfire. A married man was messing around with another lady. To spell him, his wife hexed his underwear, so that when he next had sex with the woman, she would be "rotten to the core"—a euphemism for, well, use your imagination. The problem was that the wife slept with the man before he slept with the other woman. Therefore, she was the one jinxed forever with what others swore was a rotten smell forever emanating from between her legs.

Playin' Possum

A man died and everyone was convinced that he had been done in by friends and/or relatives. To catch the culprits, they were told to put three possums in the grave. This they did. As the possums died, their spirits were released. By the end of three weeks, "shore-nuff" (as we say here in the South), three different relatives or friends of the man were dead themselves.

Grannies: Community healers who use herbal medicines for remedies; they are not root doctors.

Many people worry that the history and heritage of voodoo will be lost if it is not quickly preserved; it would indeed be a shame to lose this remarkable story of the spectrum of spirituality cum voodoo/hoodoo right here in America's own backyard. Since so many traditions were shared orally, thus the quotation:

"Each time an elder dies, a library closes."
-African proverb

Grave decorations: The tradition of placing items the deceased may have recently used on his or her grave. Items might include everything from bottles, pots, pans, eyeglasses and other such personal items, to telephones, toasters, sewing machines and televisions. Items are generally broken, perhaps to represent the death of a person in this lifetime. Some graves are decorated with a double row of conch shells to actually keep the spirit confined to the gravesite. Here at Palmetto Bluff, we have an African American cemetery, replete with grave decorations for older graves, as well as when new burials occur today.

Graveyard dirt: While it might seem like this should be free, it's apparently best to pay for it with whiskey and silver dimes.

"Green for green and brown for brown": A highly-frowned upon system where some providers of roots and herbs use almost anything of the right color as a substitute for an authentic root or herb. In other words, you might order a fairly pricy root and end up with a baggie of mulch!

Gris-gris bag: (Also spelled grigri, and sometimes also "Gregory" or "gerregery") A voodoo talisman or amulet originating in Africa; worn to protect you from evil or to bring luck.

Gullah: A term possibly derived from Angola, on the southwest coast of Africa; indicates people who came from West Africa on slave ships to the ports of Charleston or Savannah who have remained in the Lowcountry. The Gullah people refer to voodoo as 'the root.' Their beliefs include herbalism, spiritualism, and black magic.

Gullah Festival: Held in Beaufort, SC, on the weekend before Memorial Day each year.

Gullah/Geechee Cultural Preservation Act: Passed in 2006, with the goal of preserving the unique culture of the thousands of people living on St. Helena Island in the Lowcountry of South Carolina.

Gullah Glossary

Terms you may find used in conjuring, or at the local Publix grocery store. This English-based Creole language is what the Gullah of the Lowcountry so liltingly speak.

B'fo dayclean: before dawn
Bukra or buckuh: white people
Dark the light: sunset
Dayclean: dawn
Don' pit mout' on me: don't give me bad luck
Hudu: bring someone bad luck
Pull off my hat: I had to run
Sa'leenuh: St. Helena Island
Skay'd: scared

Gullah Jack: A conjureman who led a revolt at a plantation on the Stono River near Charleston, South Carolina.

Gullah, roots: Came from Angola, Gambia, Liberia, Nigeria and Senegal to the New World via slave ships to the ports of Charleston and Savannah.

Gullah Wisdom

Never have a baby in a hospital beside a graveyard. If you do, the first breath a baby tries to take will be stolen by a spirit, which will take its soul.

Salt all four corners of your new home with sea salt to keep it safe from spirits.

Gunpowder: Almost anything can come in handy in voodoo-ing. To keep a guard dog vicious, feed it gunpowder-infused cornbread. For gambling luck, put a pinch in black cow's milk and wash your hands in it. You can also mix it with success oils and keep it in your cash register to draw money to you. Note: I never thought of Blackbeard as a root doctor, but he was known to put gunpowder in the pirate grog he served to his crew.

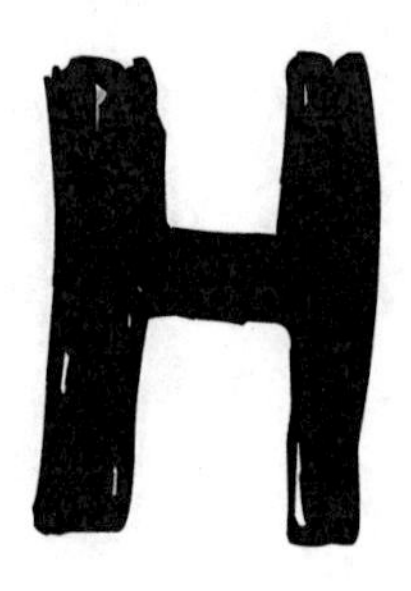

Hag: A problematic spirit. It is claimed that you can't speak when they 'ride' you and that they may ride you night after night until you are worn down. They may drive you into a screaming frenzy, but you will not actually be making any noise. Hags enter homes through a chimney or keyhole and ride you as you sleep. A hag can roost on a bedpost, lamp or other object and remain there even in daylight. It may take a root doctor to eliminate the hag, or if you are able to touch them, they may withdraw on their own. It is said they feel like a piece of raw meat and that you cannot catch them.

Hag hag: A hag that is totally a spirit, meaning it has no physical properties.

Hag stirrups: Knots in a horse's mane made by a hag.

Hag Story

"A hag will ride you. I know. One rode me one time! It was out Lands End Road. I was riding in the car with my friend. The hairs stood up on the back of my neck, and I felt something enter our car. My friend felt it too. We prayed 'The Lord is My Shepherd' and I felt my feet rise up for no reason.

"Now a hag is an old person in the neighborhood, it is said; they try to ride your back and get the life out of you for them. At home in bed, I felt that hag pounce on me and ride my back. I called my grandma and asked her what to do. She said to put a broom by the bedroom door and salt all around. I did this and the hag finally left me alone. I am a professional woman, but I swear this happened to me."

Haint blue: A color often used on doors, window frames and other parts of a house to ward off spirits. In the colonial era, this blue 'paint' was made by slaves from the leftover dye from indigo pots. The dye was quite poisonous. When I built my Savannah townhouse in the Historic District, I instinctually painted my front door a particular shade of blue. Likewise, I installed that same color Italian tile in the sun room foyer, as well as on the fireplace surround. I also selected the same color stone for my kitchen cabinet and island countertops. My first visitor was a local Lowcountry woman. She swooned, "Haint blue! Haint blue!" Thinking she was saying "Ain't blue," I looked around confused. She explained that my new special color was 'haint blue,' a shade believed to protect one against bad things and bad people. On my first night in my new home, in the 100-year-old Derst bread factory, as soon as I turned out the lights, there was the strongest odor of fresh-baking bread, which ebbed away after about twenty minutes or so. I could only assume that the 'haints' were happy with me.

Haints, hants: (noun) Angry spirits that can pass through something as small as a keyhole. Once inside, they may rattle chains, slam doors, or levitate furniture. Watch for them on full moon nights. Haints can be found around the world, but they especially favor Lowcountry swamps, wetlands, and woods.

Half-Pint Flask: A short story by Charleston author DuBose Heyward. In this tale, a plateye spirit of a former lover torments a man almost to commiting suicide. In real life, people have been known to actually kill themselves.

Hand: Another word for Mojo Bag.

Hant: (verb) To haunt, as in "He hanted his brother after his death."

Herbal medicine: Remember that in these remote Lowcountry islands, African diseases (unknown in the New World) called for cures brought from Africa. Other ailments might include lesser seen diseases such as scurvy and beriberi, as well as such diseases as syphilis, tuberculosis, and the ordinary hookworm. Slaves and freed slaves often had no medical resource or recourse other than the 'old way' cure attempts via herbs and roots.

Herbalism: A form of herbal medicine.

Herbs and roots: Along with a few animal curios and minerals, herbs and roots are the most important ingredients in hoodoo, used for oils, powders, incenses, washes, perfumes, mojo hands, voodoo dolls, spell bottles, and tricks laid down to be walked over; it is for this reason Lowcountry conjures are known as 'root doctors.'

Hex Mex

What weird machinations do hexes produce? Here's a random sampling: crawling; barking; howling; walking around naked; mooing; slobbering; fits; head whipping.

Hex Cure I: Make not one, but two, conjure

bags of ground rattlesnake rattles; wear them in your armpits.

Hex Cure II: Get one hank of hair; stand beside a willow tree; drill a hole in the willow; insert the hair; plug it with a willow twig; this supposedly cures asthma.

Hex Cure III: Take hair from the tail of a horse; soak it in corn whiskey; wash out your eyes to cure the "slobbering fits."

Hex Cure IV: Nine baths in a mixture of water, salt and baking soda, followed by a dose of iodine and potash and a rub-down with olive oil was said to have cured a man from grinding his teeth and convulsions.

Hex Cure V: Make a salve of lard rendered from a buzzard's carcass to cure leg stiffness.

High John the Conquerer: (Pronounce it KONKER.) This bulbous brown root came to hoodoo via Native American herb magic. (The Iroquois called it Manroot.) In conjuring, this root is used to command power, money, love and luck.

High magic: Hoodoo is not just the purview of the rural or semi-illiterate. Many urban root workers are highly-educated and urbane, often well-versed in the global history of such things and users of cutting edge tools of conjuring, including websites and the Internet.

"hippity-hoppity hearts": What Dr. Bug was said to have given young World War II recruits to help them foil the draft and not have to go to war.

Honey jar: A spell that uses sweeteners such as honey, syrup, molasses, etc. with a candle to compel someone to favor you or your position in court matters.

Hoo Says?

Interesting hoodoo quotes or comments:

"A hant is as natural as a man with britches."

"Boy, why you want mess around wif dat stuff?"

"Pins are used to carve names on candles, pin things together, or stab things."

"Red onions are only powerful if you steal them."

"Salt does what you tell it to."

"I don't want no jealous woman, great God, makin' up my bed; Man, she'll put something in the mattress, make you wish you was dead." "Country Woman"; recorded by Will Batts in Memphis, Tennessee in 1933

Hoodoo: Lowcountry term for voodoo; a synonym for rootwork or voodoo.

Hoodoo drugstore: Also known as "conjure shops," early 20th century spiritual supplies shops popped up following the move by some root workers from rural areas to towns. Since they could no longer grow their own roots and herbs, they often depended on these, at first, brick and mortar stores, and later, mail order and Internet sources. In 1965, Doc Miller's Rexall Drugstore in downtown Atlanta became (at the request of local patrons) a source of natural remedies and spiritual supplies. You can obtain Florida Water, used for spiritual healings, a Make Man Stay Close Spell Kit, and much more. Visit their website at medicinesandcurios.com. I plan to order the Road Opener Spell Kit, in hopes of getting all the potholes in Beaufort County repaired, and the Drive Away Evil Bath and Floor Wash—I have a new puppy. (Wish I'd named her Voodoo!) You can also order graveyard dirt and black salt. The offerings are many, and indeed, magickle!

Hoodoo You Do?

It's impossible to overstate the powerful beliefs that voodoo can inspire. Some people who have been "rooted" resort to suicide to escape what they fear may befall them. Dr. Bug was once arrested for helping Gullah draftees fail their physicals and avoid fighting during World War II. In a more modern era, some believe that Gulf War Syndrome is the result of a hex performed by none other than Saddam Hussein.

Hoodoo You Think You Are?: If I were a Boo-Hag...dada, dada, dada, dum: all night long I'd diddy diddy dum, haunting while I hum, if I were a Boo-boo Hag!

Hoppin' John: A traditional New Year's Day dish made from rice, black eyed peas, and greens; these give you good luck and money in the coming year.

Hot Footing: A spell or ritual to drive away an enemy or some other person causing you problems.

Houngan: Voodoo priest/priestess; some say they steal the souls of dead people and turn them into them zombies who do their will.

How do you hoodoo?: It's important to understand that hoodoo, herb magic, folk magic, etc. go way back in time. When Africans were brought to America as slaves, they brought beliefs and customs with them that were unique to hoodoo. Some of these included the use (in 'rooting') of spice plants, stinging insects, certain metals, and mineral salts, as well as special significance of the dead, graveyards, crossroads, doorsteps, foot tracks, amulets, and the number nine.

Hush-hush: For many years, recollection of, and even belief in and practice of, voodoo was intentionally kept quiet and out of sight. Blacks feared white retribution at their determination to continue to practice their old ways, especially since voodoo activities continued to some degree, even to the present. However, these days, festivals and celebrations of the Gullah ways are now held and participated in by blacks and whites alike, including surprised and bewildered tourists.

I

Ifa: If there was a ground zero of African cultural traditions that made their way to the New World, it was from the Yoruba nation (present day Nigeria). The Yorubas and their cultural beliefs, called *Ifa*, came ashore to form the early basis for what would become a voodoo heritage that continues to this day in the Lowcountry.

Indian Scouts: The Indian head cents go by this name. Since they have not been minted since 1909, they may be a bit hard to find. However, if you can locate some, they can be nailed around door frames or across your threshold to keep the police, IRS, and other forms of law away. One old building in the South had 1,500 'scouts' nailed around the premises.

Indigo blue: The original name of the color 'haint blue'; first obtained from the leftovers in the pots of dye made from the indigo plant; believed to ward off evil spirits; often used on doors and window shutters.

Ingredients: While this book would be 1,000 pages long if it included all the spells and stories of Lowcountry voodoo, here are a few curious ingredients essential for just a few spells: black cat bone to gain invisibility; black hen's egg to suss out a murderer (or to stop baby teething pain); rattlesnake for acquiring a musical skill; raccoon penis bone for luck in gambling; coffin nails to jinx someone; menstrual blood (in food) to keep a man; bat's blood to write pacts (heed this lawyers!); five fingered grass to cleanse and purify; wormwood in a bag hung from a rearview mirror to prevent accidents; Four Thieves Vinegar for protection; and graveyard dirt/tobacco snuff/sugar to draw trade to a whorehouse. There are many more...many, many more!

Instructions: A conjure or a gris-gris bag always comes with instructions of what you are to do next. Women usually pin the charm inside their bra or under their shirt near their left armpit. Men wear the bag around the neck or pinned inside their underwear, or even in a pocket, where it can be freely and frequently fondled. I knew a man who liked to grow tiny pumpkins and put them in his farm jeans front pockets and fondle them; often, he would startle mothers when he pulled a tiny pumpkin from his pocket to present to their delighted children.

irin ajo: A spiritual journey, from the former Yoruba Empire's Ifa religion. Devotees seek to unite earthly consciousness through oneness with all Creation, a system of ethics, religious belief, and mystic vision. Ancestral spirits help in the journey to spiritual destiny, or *ayanmo*.

Jack Mullater: Also called Jack-o-Lantern or ghost light; a hag that carries a lantern. You can often spy such hags on Lands End Road on St. Helena Island. You're most apt to see them in the swamp where high concentrations of phosphorescence can be found. At night, this soup of dirt, leaves, fungi, rotted stumps, decayed trees, and other decaying organic matter glows, even floating through the air as a ball.

Jasmine: The Jessamine vine adorns many a Lowcountry arbor. Jasmine oil is said to aid a person to have psychic dreams.

J. E. (Ed) McTeer

In 1926, at the age of 22, Ed McTeer was sworn in to fill the role of Beaufort County sheriff left vacant after his father's death. Called the "boy sheriff" by some whites, the Gullah called him the High Sheriff. Ed had been surrounded by voodoo culture from the time he was born. To govern effectively, he showed respect for the black culture as well as the white and kept a kind of peace that was rather uncommon in the South during those pre-civil rights years. Not content with merely researching the ancient traditions, Ed himself became a practitioner of roots.

He was to the "spiritual manor born," you could say. He'd heard tales of such things from his grandfather. His grandmother was a medium and spiritualist. As a child he recalled a seance she conducted, during which the heavy dining room table shook beneath his grandmother's hands. Ed also believed in ESP, which he called "second sight." He further believed such skills were inherited and a very dear thing to be cultivated, not scorned.

As High Sheriff, he encountered many a strange thing: sudden deaths with no cause; strangers in the courtroom, clearly there only to give the evil eye to anyone who might testify inappropriately; white "powders" drizzled on the judge's desk; and more. Clearly, Ed had a lot to learn. Learn, he did, and was such a fan of Lowcountry voodoo that in his later years you might find him spreading his own roots and other wares out on a school cafeteria table for the perusal of the kitchen staff. In his home at Coffin Point, he kept a voodoo altar, and liked to pose beside it in photos.

During a challenge to his office by a South Carolina highway patrol sergeant, a planned televised debate (a big deal in the 1960s) fizzled out in a blaze of screen snow, just as if a root or hex had been cast upon the program hour. Beaten by a small margin, Ed retired to write his memoirs–*Fifty Years as a Low Country Witch Doctor*.

And the new sheriff? Well, whether rooted or not, he was soon out of office after a debacle of assault, suicide threats and more.

McTeer died in 1976. Who carries on his rootwork? If it were you, would you tell?

Job: Another term for a spell.

Johnny Jump-Up: Not surprisingly, this type of common violet is used to make men more potent.

Juniper: A common shrub in the Lowcountry; some ships were made with juniper wood. But in voodoo-doin's, the berries are used for all kinds of sexual issues. Just one of these uses is as a vaginal douche (commonly called Hot Mama Douche), presumably to make men hot and bothered.

Just Rooting Around

A few things you might find in Lowcountry retail outlets that sell such items:

Adam and Eve Herb
Hearts Cologne
Love Balm
St. John the Conqueror
Success Oil
Zoological Curios, like Alligator Claws

King of the root world: High John the Conqueror (often spelled Conker), especially when 'dressed' with Hearts Cologne and prayer.

Kodak moment: Never let your photo be taken. Why? Because the camera will steal your soul.

Kuwfa: A dead person.

Lady hearted: A root worker or spiritual practitioner morally opposed to harming a person or animal through the use of spells or magick.

"Leettle chair": A St. Helena Island man believed that he had been visited by a plateye spirit after it came through the wall of his dead daughter's room and sat in her "leettle chair." He felt this happened because he had failed to get the advice of a root doctor during her extended illness.

Legal or Illegal?

- There is no law in South Carolina against casting or removing spells.

- However, if a root doctor dispenses a salve, body oil or potion, he can be cited for practicing medicine without a license.

Lemon: Lowcountry Sicilians (if there are such things) stab a lemon with nine nails that are then wound with red thread. This charm is used above a door to protect against envy. Early English folk just put their lemons up the chimney.

Lemon Grass: A tropical grass unrelated to lemon. Used to ward off evil messes and "crossed conditions." A major ingredient in Van Van Oil, Hindu Grass Oil and Henry's Grass Oil. Note: We have a Peaceful Henry cigar shop here in Bluffton, where I live; I do not think they sell Lemon Grass.

Licorice: While licorice is used for flavoring, medically it is a demulcent and expectorant. It contains phytoestrogens and also affects blood pressure. Voodoo-aly, it is said to help you control a person or situation. You can Dress a Room for Commanding People There…make a Love-Controlling Mojo… create Domination Incense…and use licorice with Essence of Bend-Over Oil, for exactly what purpose, I do not wish to know.

Life Everlasting: Also called Life Alasses, this chest rub is made from whiskey, lemon and turpentine. A tea from leaves, stems, and flowers of the Life Everlasting plant could also be made. For asthma, you could smoke the dried plant. For toothache, chew the crumbled leaves. A bath in it could cure foot pain and skin ailments.

Little John to Chew: If a person chews Little John and spits the juice on the floor of the courtroom, legal matters will go in their favor, especially if the judge happens to step in the juice. While this may fly in an early Lowcountry courtroom, today you may have to resort to spitting Little John in your hand and rubbing it on the court pews.

Live Things

One of the most fearful spells is the introduction of "live things" (snakes, spiders, and such) into or beneath the skin of a person.

History: Belief in wild things in your body came from Native American and African American cultures. Supposedly, if you were secretly fed certain animal parts, you would end up suffering from live creatures writhing in your body. Witnesses have sworn to have seen or suffered from things visibly squirming beneath the skin. People so afflicted might also crawl on all fours, howl like a dog, or even die.

The Method: Things suitable to achieving live things in someone include frog spawn, horse hair, ground dog, lizard heads, snake eggs, shed or skin, blood from a scorpion's tail, crushed insects, powdered snails or spider eggs, concealed in dumplings. Ice cream, alas, is also a common dish to introduce such items.

The Cure: An emetic of poke root, olive oil and saltpeter will cause you to vomit up your live things, or they may be expelled from the rectum.

The Medical Explanation: Is it possible that live things are intestinal worms? Very likely, when the sufferer has abdominal pains. Some cases may be untreated diabetic neuropathy.

Obviously, sometimes, sleight-of-hand may produce a bowl full of wriggling things. In the meantime, buy your own ice cream and check those dumplings!

Loa: a god

Loading: Digging a hole in the bottom of a candle to insert herbs, oils, personal concerns, powders, or other items; and then plugging the hole.

Lodestones: Naturally occurring magnets made of magnetized pieces of the mineral magnetite. Used in spells and rituals and charms.

Love: Signs, potions and more dot the Gullah belief landscape: To get more admirers, burn your ex-lover's shoes. Pin a piece of your lover's shirt to your skirt to ensure they remain faithful. If you dream of a gray horse, pick out your wedding dress!

Love Potion Number Nine: In hoodoo parlance, this is a dressing oil; once it was primarily an herb tea you drank for nine days, preferably homemade and infused with rose petals, red clover and catnip and steeped in hot water for nine minutes.

Lowcountry: The low-lying coastal areas of South Carolina, Georgia and upper Florida. While this includes the Sea Islands, technically, the Lowcountry in South Carolina also encompasses all areas below the state's fall line.

Lucky Mojo Curio Company: It's just easier to share their own stated reason for being… *Lucky Mojo is both an online magic shop and a real magic store that you can visit. We carry a full line of hand-made spiritual supplies, including occult oils, incense, powders, candles, herbs, mojo bags, spiritual soaps, books, and spell kits for those who cast magic spells, love spells, money spells, and protection spells in the African-American hoodoo, Pagan magick, and other Witchcraft traditions. We also import and distribute folkloric, magical, occult, herbal, and spiritual supplies from Asia, Latin America, and the Middle East for those who work in Hindu, Buddhist, Catholic, Protestant, Muslim, and Jewish religious and magical traditions. We sell retail and wholesale, both on the Internet and at our old-timey, small-town occult shop.* Something for everyone? They even have a newsletter.

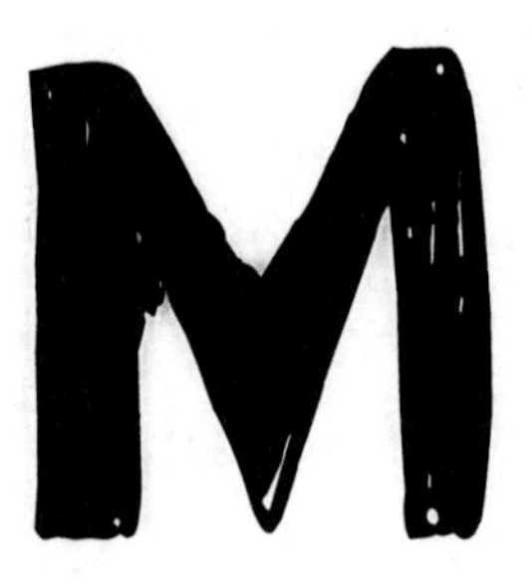

Mace: More than a police poultice, mace was once used as a "money-drawing" douche by prostitutes, who mixed the powder with distilled vinegar and water. A customer who encountered this concoction was thus in her power and under her control for repeated well-paid visits.

Magic: White magic is harmless, even for good; black magic is evil used to accomplish bad outcomes.

Magnetic sand: Carry some in a red flannel bag for money and good luck.

Magnolia, You Sweet Thing: After live oaks festooned with Spanish moss, nothing is more beautiful than our glossy-leafed magnolia trees awash in dinner plate-size white blooms. Via conjuration, you are able to keep a husband or wife faithful by sewing the leaves into your mattress. If you are not confident of the power of this conjure, you can also create a mojo packet of semen-smeared 'nine-knot measure' of the husband's penis, so that he is unable to perform with any other woman. Hoodoo you do, indeed.

Marie Laveau: The most famous voodoo priestess from New Orleans, active during the Civil War era. Legend has it that she would go deep into the bayou and awaken the zombies on St. John's Eve.

Max Beauvoir: Spokesman for the Houngans; a doctor's son, he left Haiti to attend college, even studying chemistry at the Sorbonne. When he returned home, his father made him promise to take over his job as a voodoo priest.

McTeer Method

In the 1960s, Beaufort County Sheriff Ed McTeer gave a talk to a civic group, sharing this story:

An old Gullah woman had been hexed by a very evil root. She had "wizened and waned" and was near death. McTeer came to her house to perform an exorcism. He moved the weak woman out into the yard and gathered her family and friends around. Donning his special haint blue sunglasses, the sheriff announced that he was going to use his mighty conjuring powers to cure the woman. Entering into a trance, McTeer's arms and legs began to tremble as he walked around the yard, head tossed back. He began to speak in tongues. Suddenly–as all stared in awe–he bolted for the dirt beneath the steps and plucked out a nasty blue root, the source of the evil! Amid praise and applause, the unofficial root doctor returned home. A subsequent visit a week later found the woman out and about, cooking and cleaning like her old self.

The method? McTeer confessed that he had previously planted the offending root beneath the steps. This method worked for him many times, saving lives, time, money and suffering, and garnering him many votes in future elections!

How to cancel a blue root's power:

- Toss it into the flowing waters of a tidal creek
- Burn it in a fiery stove

Men, beware!: This has to be the all-time oddest root potion, period. No, literally—*period.* Women, eager to get men to marry them, would cook delicious dishes, such as red rice, and add a special secret ingredient. You guessed it—their menstrual fluids.

Minerva: Voodoo priestess; character in John Berendt's best-selling novel, *Midnight in the Garden of Good and Evil*, set in Savannah, Georgia. Based on a real-life hoodoo practitioner.

Mojo: As in "Get yo' mojo on!" A magic charm, talisman, or spell; magical powers.

Money: There are many signs the Gullah believe that predict money is either headed your way...or out of your hand: Right hand itch? Only a letter is coming. Left hand itch? Money is coming! A red bird on your doorstep means money will come to you. So do bubbles in your coffee. If you dream of running water, you will gain money and good fortune, both.

Mouthing: Chewing a root, without the actual root. You do not have to chew in the presence of your victim. Used to confer bad luck, rather than death or illness, other than perhaps headache or extreme irritability.

Myth or Magic?

So what is actually going on in rootland? Is it myth, magic, meanness, imagination, something else?

The "law of similarity" says "like produces like." For example, when a mockingbird sat upon Dr. Buzzard's head, it is not a giant leap to associate this aggressive, mimicking bird with human antics and endeavors.

The "law of contact" maintains that objects that were once connected remain so, even if widely separated. Thus, if you snatch a bit of your lover's hair, you should be able to create a root to conjure up some trouble if he or she becomes unfaithful.

Combining roots can create all kinds of evil concoctions. While it may all seem like moonshine shenanigans or campfire tales, there are real life examples of roots and hexes, even attacking hags, bringing about death to those afflicted with such a curse.

Limited, but compelling, scientific experiments with rats have shown that if convinced that death is imminent, a rat—or person—can will themselves to die. Examples in humans include a cascade failure of the sympathetic nervous system that can result in heart failure and death.

Emotions and beliefs matter. Dying of a broken heart is possible. You can be "scared to death" for sure. Of a hellish hex? If you know you've been conjured, and are suddenly covered with boils and sores and such...hmm.

As I've always claimed: Truth is stranger than fiction!

May the Hex [not] be with you!

Name papers/Petition papers: Small pieces of paper with peoples' names, symbols, or phrases of intent written on them for use in the practice of voodoo. They are primarily placed beneath candles, tucked into shoes, included in mojo bags, or used in bottle spells. Pencil is OK, but can be erased; red ink is good; green ink can be used for money matters. It is said that you can also use dragon, bat, or dove blood ink. If that seems like a lot of trouble, be aware that the paper should be from a brown grocery sack that has not been machine cut; parchment paper is ok, too. You also need conditioning oil to 'fix' the paper. How you write the name is critical, also. 'Crossing and covering' is writing the name three times one way, then over that, three times the other way. There are folding procedures, then more fixing procedures, then placing procedures. And I thought writing this book was hard.

Names, cool: It seems that our Lowcountry conjure land is full of charming names: Rumpetty Dick, Meat-Skin Martin, Jorico Pope, Hot-Bread-Cut Jack Warren, and such.

Native Americans and African Americans: Early in Lowcountry history, the native Indians and the newly brought slaves had interactions where they shared special herbal methods, including the use of raccoon penis bones and tobacco in rituals and spells.

New Year's Day: The popular January 1 traditions that many people in the South faithfully adhere to came from Gullah culture. Be sure to eat collard greens, roast pork, and Hoppin' John for good luck all year. The greens bring you paper money; the peas, coins. This may sound familiar, also…after the dishes are cleared, place a dollar bill and a silver dollar on the table. Put a green candle on top. Around these, place leftover pork, greens, and Hoppin' John. Use salt and seasonings to inscribe a circle around all this. Light the candle and say prayers for prosperity. Leave it all in place overnight. The next morning, toss it all out to avoid bad luck.

Numbers-I: In hoodoo, the numbers three and nine have great significance.

Numbers-II: How many Gullah are still in existence? It has been estimated that around 150,000 are still living in the Lowcountry of South Carolina and (as Geechee) in the coastal areas of Georgia.

Numbers Game: There should never be an even number of charms in a gris-gris or other bag, nor more than 13 items. So that leaves you 1, 3, 5, 7, 9, 11 or 13 items to conjure with.

Old Sheldon Church, Yemassee, SC: Beautiful, but haunting, Lowcountry icon of the ruins of a brick and tabby church and graveyard. The church was destroyed twice during the American Revolution by the British, as well as by General Sherman during the U.S. Civil War. Popular and highly-photographic site for weddings and family reunions.

Oral tradition: African Americans have a rich oral heritage. For this reason, memories of their original homelands, traditions and culture came ashore with them intact and ready to take root in the New World. Whether it was spiritual or religious beliefs, skills, songs or stories, all were passed down through generations including to the present. Perhaps once misunderstood or even ridiculed, today the Gullah-Geechee and other such cultures are considered fascinating, historical, prized, and worth exploring and preserving.

Orunmila: The Moses of the Ifa faith; his name translates to "Only Heaven Knows the Way to Salvation." Orunmila, from a remote village, was a sickly child, referred to as a little boy with a big head. According to legend, Orunmila was tutored by sixteen elders sent to Earth by God. These angelic beings helped the boy become divine. Orunmila collected the basic truths which originated with the origin of the world. The Yoruba believe that Ifa is the original religion of earthly humans. As the religion spread from Africa outward, it became obvious that many tenets of the faith reflected those of the Ten Commandments.

"Ouch!": Believe it or not, colored pins are required for your voodoo doll. Map pins with colored heads are fine to use.

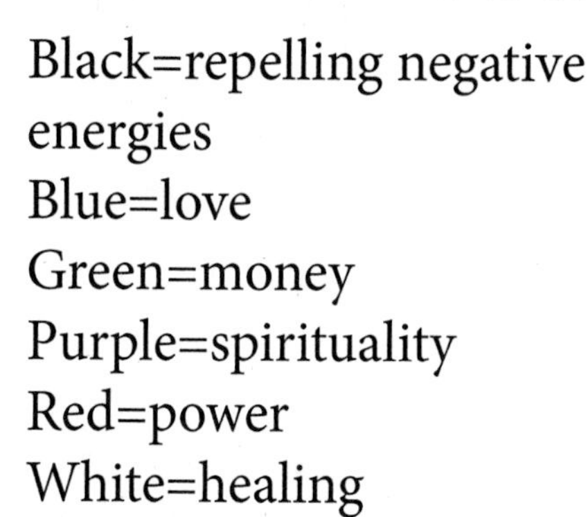

Black=repelling negative energies
Blue=love
Green=money
Purple=spirituality
Red=power
White=healing
Yellow=success

Ouija hoodoo: The American tradition of primarily young girls using a Ouija board to contact 'spirits' and asking questions—mostly about boys!

Owl, to quiet one: A hooting owl is a bad omen. Here's how to get one to hush up: Cross your fingers; take off a shoe and turn it over. Point your finger in the direction of the hooting sound. Put a poker in the fire. Squeeze your right wrist with your left hand. Got it?

Oyotunji: African word for 'rise again.'

Passin' the chirrun: Gullah tradition of handing children back and forth over the coffin or grave of a loved one so that the spirits would not later return to haunt them.

Passing the mantle: The transferring of knowledge and power from one conjurer or root doctor to an apprentice, perhaps a son.

'Personal Concerns': This curious euphemism refers to, well, things personal to a person for use in conjure work. Just a few 'items' that fall into this general category include (in no particular order): semen, vaginal fluids, menstrual blood, urine, feces, bathwater, pubic hair, armpit hair, sweat, spit, fingernails, toenails, skin, baby teeth, handwriting, names, and body part measurements.

Pins and Needles: While it seems like a straight pin or sewing needle should be sufficient to effect pain via a voodoo doll, other choices include yucca plant (Spanish Bayonet) spikes, coffin nails, cactus, or similar sharp objects… say an ice pick?

Google "1,000 voodoo dolls" and you will soon find that takes you to PINTEREST, which does indeed feature all kinds of (actually, perfectly adorable, often gingerbready-looking) voodoo dolls. And now you know why they call it PINterest!

Pirates and voodoo: It is well-known that pirates, such as Blackbeard (called the "fiercest of them all"), often headed to the barrier islands of North or South Carolina to bury their ill-gotten treasure. Their regular ruse was to kill the lowly buccaneers assigned to the burial detail and bury them over the dead man's chest of booty. It is said that these men often became 'plateyes,' spirits who rose up to chase away anyone who came near the suspicious site. Sometimes they appeared as a headless hog, six-legged calf, or other animal.

Plateye: Spirit believed to have returned from the spirit world to do mischief (perhaps at the bidding of the root doctor), or to engage in revenge against someone who has wronged them. A shape-shifter, it can change forms to suit the situation. Plateyes usually take the form of a large dog, bear or horse. Plateyes favor the Lowcountry because of the endless swamps, fields and woods. A plateye may have been sent to hound you by a root doctor. Plateyes can often be placated by offering them whiskey, their weakness. A bit of bourbon poured on the ground may distract the spirit long enough for you to make your escape, or, if you are brave, stand your ground and say the Lord's Prayer aloud.

Poisoned through the feet: When a person has walked over or stepped on magickal powder laid down in their path to affect them in a negative way.

Power of suggestion: Do not underestimate the power of suggestion in voodoo. Charms, amulets, rings, talismans, religious objects, effigies, or magical formulas are often considered by psychiatrists as 'preventive' when they are of a positive nature. Medical missionaries note that many primitive people will take a written prescription and wear it around their neck—and get as much benefit as if they had actually taken the medicine—possibly because such a measure is more compatible with the person's belief system.

Power of the root: Exhibits in many ways; one example is the writhing imminent death of a person, presumably brought on by being 'rooted' by neighbors, perhaps due to some disagreement, such as over property lines; or an instance of aggravation like animals allowed to chow down on someone else's garden. The spell is cast, the hags ride, and there is often little to counter the eventual demise of the person, nor to quite separate fact from folklore.

Praise houses: Small, plain chapels built on plantations so that slaves could worship as they pleased. Pews were rough pine benches; preaching was often eloquent and harked back to Africa tribal traditions. From a window you might have heard the sound of 'the shout' hymns of praise. Today you can still see original praise houses on St. Helena Island, hear 'shout,' and be blessed if you are welcomed to any such service.

Presider: A ward (similar to a bishop); is highly respected.

Quassia: (Also known as bitter ash, bitter wood, bitter room or Quassia Amara) This is a bitter tonic; in concentrated form it may be used in insecticides. In voodoo, it is used to control a lover. For example, quassia chips may be burned to ash and mixed with your lover's hair or other personal concerns to control them.

Queen Elizabeth Root: Also called the love root, this fragrant iris is said to be used by women and gay men to attract male lovers. It is powerful enough to help you obtain a marriage proposal, a man's love, control over a man, excite a man, and other passionate responses. You can also use the root, threaded with red thread, as a pendulum for divination. Best kept in a red flannel bag when not in use.

Rattlesnake Round Up: The use of rattlesnakes in folk magic dates back to pre-Columbian times. Admirably, hoodooers are conscientious about not killing snakes for their rattles during 'round-ups' when the snakes are hibernating. Snake sheds are good to use, as are 'roadkill' rattlers. You can also substitute Rattlesnake Grass.

Reader: A root worker or spiritual practitioner who is psychically gifted.

Reasons for consulting practitioners of voodoo: Almost any practical day-to-day need—health matters, revenge, hopes for success, emotional needs, and more.

Reason for Roots

Roots are more than physical things like herbs or bones. It is the combination of these along with magical words, specific intentions, and utter belief that is supposed to lead to achieving desired goals: success in business; luck in love; a cure for an illness; protection of a loved one; the death of an enemy, just to name a few!

Reasons voodoo has persisted into this century: First slaves, then free, many African Americans still live in Lowcountry communities in a close-knit culture, some in more isolated areas. This has preserved much of their original native beliefs, language, and culture to this day. Indeed, a good bit of tourism is tied to fascination in this colorful part of American history. Folklorists, linguists, historians, anthropologists and others devote much time to documenting and preserving this history. Locals and visitors enjoy tours and annual celebrations. Writers and publishers, authors and artists, musicians and craftspeople revel in this remarkably preserved history and culture.

Recipe for a Charm

Here's an example of the elaborate ritual of a Love Charm. Remember, this is for information only...if you don't believe, it won't work; if you aren't a professional conjurer, maybe you should just read, not try.

Ingredients:

1 red bride and groom candle
Anointing oil, such as jasmine, lavender or virgin olive oil
Incense, like frankincense or rose petals
Bath crystals
Sachet powder
A pair of lodestones
A pack of magnetic sand
A packet of herbs, such as spikenard and damiana
John the Conqueror root
Queen Elizabeth root
Red flannel bag
String tie for bag
Heart charm
Personal item from you
Personal item from the person you desire

Note: Try to get the "Love Me" brand of most of these products

Ritual Preparation:

Day One: In a dark, quiet room, have only altar candles burning as a light source. Bathe in a bath of the crystals; fill a jug with the bathwater and save it. Sprinkle sachet powder on your body and inside your shoes, also in the four corners of your room and between the mattress and box spring. Dress in clean clothes and go outside. Throw the jug of bathwater to the east; turn around and walk back home; do not look back. While performing these things, say special words of your own choosing. [Save and divide the ingredients to use in subsequent days' rituals.]

Day One and Each Day:
Light the incense in a burner; write your name and your desired's name on the bride and groom candle. Rub the sides of the candle with anointing oil. Place the lodestones nearby. Into the red flannel bag, put the sachet powder, roots, and

sand. Chant a few words of your choice; tie the bag with the string. Each day, coat the lodestones with the magnetic sand and move them a bit closer to each other. On the seventh day, they should be touching one another. Snuff out the candle and incense; put the stones in the bag, add love oil and carry all around with you until the charm takes effect.

Final Day:
Save all remaining materials; put in a small bag or piece of cloth; add a piece of paper with your name and your desired's name on it; tie the bag tightly and bury it in your yard. Say a few words of love over it to complete the charm. Wait for the charm to work!

Note: This is sort of an average charm; many are far more elaborate, requiring trips to graveyards at midnight, and, perhaps the boiling of a cat and grinding up of its thigh bone.

Reddening: Red brick dust used in spells.

Red Devil: A commercial brand of lye commonly used as a spiritual cleaning agent by dusting an 'eviled' doorstep. You can also bury it "as deep as your pillow" beneath a gate to keep evil out of your yard. Note: Add nine ten-penny nails or nine new straight pins for extra protection.

Ring shouts: Tight circles of early African American worshipers dancing in unison as they sang in a religious ecstasy of clapping and foot stomping to the tune of drums and tambourines.

Ritual: Something you do before you seal your gris-gris bag or perform some other root or charm. Can include chanting, praying, singing and such. This can be done while you watch, or the root doctor may do this out of your sight, and then give you the bag with instructions of what to do next.

Root-I: Can be an actual herb or plant, but also a charm, mojo, gris-gris, or hand carried, worn, chewed or buried, depending on the objective it is supposed to achieve. Roots can be purchased or custom-made.

Root-II: The root is a charm, mojo, or gris-gris. Most roots are small cloth sacks or liquids stored in small vials. Roots can be worn, chewed, buried or carried. They can be traditional or custom-made. Roots can be administered or removed only by a root doctor. You can 'root' someone, or be 'rooted.' I suppose if a hex or spell is reversed, you can be 'unrooted' or 'derooted.' If you are determined to visit the environs of Lowcountry voodoo, your GPS will 'reroot' you down local roads to places such as St. Helena Island and Coffin Point.

Root doctor: Traditionally, someone who practices voodoo with the use of roots, herbs, spells, even hexes—but not medicine.

Root Doctor Redux

How do you find a root doctor? Not on the Internet or through the Yellow Pages. Word of mouth is the best bet. Best that you be a believer in such things, and not tempted to threaten to sue if you are not totally pleased with results. It's probably not the best idea to make your Dr. Root angry! And where would you find Dr. Root? Not via a business card, Google search, or GPS. Follow the yellow brick mailbox! Ask, then ask again. Eventually someone may direct you to a remote barrier island, or a shed office down a dirt lane, or a street corner. Be prepared to answer a lot of questions...and ask none.

Visit to a root doctor: What might you encounter? Perhaps a shabby office, dark, except for a single burning candle. You surreptitiously survey the doctor's desk, spying a peculiar array of this and that: wax, twigs, snippets of cloth, notes with indecipherable scrawls, and such. "Have a seat," Dr. Root insists. Dare you?

Being read: How does a root doctor suss out your essence, your need, your truth, your fear? He will take your hand in his and manipulate each bone, each sinew. Whatever he asks, you will answer truthfully, won't you? He will ask questions; he may give answers.

Business as (un)usual: How are fees charged? Everything on the dollar spectrum from free to as fantastically expensive as a trial lawyer. Paying up in advance is standard. How do you pay Dr. Root? You won't get a bill; you can't use a credit card. You will get a slip of paper with an amount written on it. Note that the good doctor has not asked you to pay up. But you do.

Root doctors are ready when you are!

Once, in Beaufort County, South Carolina, two "lucky" roots were requested to be rushed to the Savannah Airport, the purchasers refusing to board the plane until the roots arrived. (Obviously, this was before TSA.)

Root of All Evil: If money is the root of all evil, money accepted for medicinal herbs and roots as a cure for an illness is illegal if you are not a licensed doctor. Dr. Buzzard once tore up thousands of dollars in money orders so that there would be no evidence he had ever done such a thing—had he done it.

Rooting for the Home Team: Examples of everyday, ordinary being rooted (according to visitors to my home during the research for this book): One boy virtually went crazy when he said he was rooted and all of his perfectly good teeth began to fall out one at the time. One girl said she was rooted and cried all the time, even when she was happy; when the person who rooted her died suddenly, her tears vanished. Oh, and many, many more… trust me!

Rootwork

Examples of results of being rooted:

Fingernail + bone from a black dog = the person falls to their hands and knees, poops on the floor, and howls at the moon.

Hair + lizard bones = hallucinations of lizards crawling on you.

Skin + snake or salamander = an eruption of boils and sores.

Rootwork Recipe Round-Up: Part of the annual Conjure Cook-Off and its art of magical cooking. According to the ladies of the Missionary Independent Church, the use of hoodoo herbs also applies to cooking as a time-honored form of domestic spell magic, sometimes called 'kitchen witchery.' Recipes may promote peace and harmony, enhance romance, bless a marriage, or, on the other side of the hoodoo coin, stop office gossip or get a nasty neighbor to move away.

Root Ways and Means

"I may not believe in roots, but I no longer scoff at them."

A Beaufort attorney hired a Gullah housekeeper. She turned out to be unmotivated and he fired her. She stormed from his home swearing to "root" him. The lawyer hired a new woman. The first day on the job, she discovered three new sewing needles tied up with black thread beneath the couple's mattress. The new maid warned him that the bundle was a suffering root and that he should seek help from a root doctor immediately. Both the man and his wife scoffed at the very idea.

The next day, the wife came down with a terrible rash which turned out to be a severe case of chicken pox; the next day their baby came down with the same. Next her husband developed awful stomach pains and was rushed to the hospital to have his appendix removed. Their older son was already in the hospital to have his tonsils removed. During the operation, the boy ceased breathing and was barely revived.

The attorney then experienced many post-op infections. During a visit to the doctor, he noted the black stitches in his wound and thought of the very similar black thread and needles. He demanded the doctor remove the stitches. Reluctantly, the doctor did and the man healed. The family's cascade of suffering was ended.

As he said in the headline above, he may not believe, *nonetheless...*

Why, and how, does rooting work?

Like many things, if you believe it, it works. While we may believe that such spiritual beliefs are long in the past, not so—especially not in the Lowcountry! *Spirituality?* Most Gullah are devout

Christians. While this might seem contradictory to conjuring, note that even the Bible mentions conjurers and witches. "Any man who don't believe in witches don't believe in God," attested a Gullah preacher.

While some consider the success of rooting is through auto-suggestion, however it works, it's easy to imagine a cascade of: "I sort of believe; it may be possible; there may be something to this."...to..."I lost my job; was I hexed?"...to..."And now I've lost my wife...I have definitely been hexed."... to..."I'm calling Dr. Buzzard and putting him on speed dial!"

Rootwork is the tie that binds, a kind of kudzulike vine that entwines various beliefs, whether utterly serious or "just in case," or perhaps even just for fun, into a kind of tiered belief system, a pharmacopeia of tools for just the right need at the right time. Nor is rootwork only practiced and used by black people. Whites have their own beliefs and needs. After all, if you're hexed...who ya gonna call?!

Runs: A candle-worker's term for the practice of lighting a new candle from an old one until you get the results you desire.

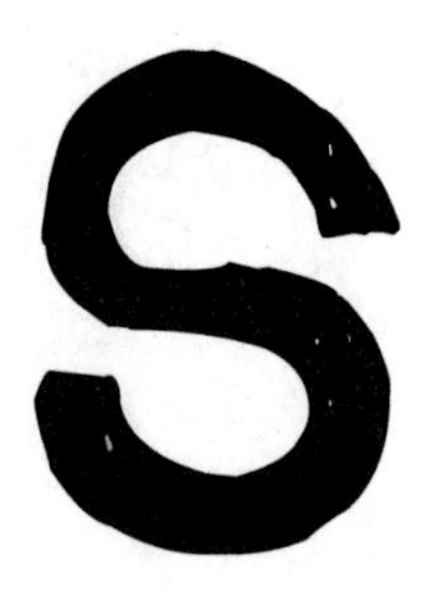

Sassafras tea: Boiled from the roots of the Life Everlasting plant, it was used as a tonic and cold remedy.

Saw off the bedposts: What you do to keep the boo hags from roosting over a person.

Sea islands: The sea islands of coastal South Carolina and Georgia are the most 'ground zero' location of surviving West African culture. Those who were forced onto slave ships bound for the New World brought no personal possessions, but instead, a wealth of legend, lore, spirituality, seeds, and knowledge from their native lands. Remnants of this culture in the form of hoodoo and voodoo still exist there today, often in a vibrant and essential way.

Seaweed: Agar-Agar, an algae, is a kind of seaweed also known as Sea Lettuce or Sea

Spirit. It is said to protect against evil spirits and also to give you semi-invisibility, whatever exactly that is. In the laboratory, it's used as a growth medium. Powdered, it serves as a food thickener.

Second burial: An African tribal practice whereby a quickly decomposed body (in the jungle heat) was left to simmer in a temporary grave for a year or so until a proper burial could take place. At that time, family and friends gathered for a feast and a respectful transfer of the exhumed bones. During this prior putrid purgatory, a spirit was often restless. No doubt.

Secrecy: Much of root work depends on great secrecy, not only of the ingredients in a root, but also the double-down power of special magic words spoken in 'unknown tongues' as the root is being prepared.

Seeking: The Gullah people insist that you must do more than just proclaim that you believe in God. You must go through a 'seeking' via the salvation of your soul. A spiritual leader will guide you through prayer, fasting, and meditation. When you have 'come tru,' you can finally be baptized.

Setting lights: Preparing a candle for an individual petition and praying over it daily until it has burned out.

Sex Hex

The power of the root, indeed...

In the 1960s, a Beaufort man wanted to divorce his wife to marry his lover. Angry, his spouse took a pair of his undershorts and sprinkled it with a white powder obtained from a root doctor; she then burned the shorts in the stove, warning her husband, "You may leave me...but you'll never be a man to that woman!" They divorced and the man remarried. However, he was never able to perform sexually and his new wife left him. He committed suicide with a shot to the head.

Shape-shifter: Synonym for a boo hag or witch.

Shouts: "The spirit moved me!" dances of praise to God often involving singing, shouting, jumping, jiggling, foot-stamping and clapping.

Shut Mouth Root: This remedy means you will no longer be bothered by whatever (or whomever) is bothering you. Secondly, you will be unable to resist telling others that you have rooted someone, in confidence, of course. Like a kid's game of Gossip, the word spreads. Eventually, but untraceable back to you, the rooted person hears the bad news. Are your problems over? Possibly. (Unless they do a reverse root on you!)

Slip-skin hag: A person (usually a woman) who becomes invisible by shedding her skin by pulling it over her head like a sweater. This kind of hag generally visits after dark but is gone by dayclean (morning). They like math, but suck at it. So plop a colander or flour sifter over a doorknob to repel them. Although they can slip through either one, if they stop to count the holes, it may stump them for so long that morning comes and they retreat. You can also sprinkle salt around your bed, in hopes of contaminating the shed skin. If you think you know who your hag is, write her name on your door along with the word HAG and she will not enter.

Spanish moss: This is neither here nor there in the land of voodoo, just an interesting fact—Lowcountry Native Americans once used Spanish moss for baby diapers and sanitary napkins. Just so you know: Spanish moss (*Tillandsia usneoides*) is not a moss, nor is it from Spain. That's just a lot of hoodoo; it's a bromeliad, which means it's in the same family as pineapples and succulent house plants. Of course, what would voodoo magic in the Garden of Good and Evil be without abundant festoons of Spanish moss? Note: Spanish moss was also used to make a tea said to relieve rheumatism, abscesses, and labor pains. Also for rooting, but most of all to stuff baby (voodoo) dolls.

Spirit animals: Although they appear as normal creatures, if they cross your path, you will feel goosebumps dot your arms and legs. These animals give off the smell of raw meat and walk with a high-stepping gait.

Spirit bears: Most common following the War Between the States, these animals were quite large, roared, and even breathed fire.

Spirit types: Spirits may be the souls released from dead bodies. But in voodoo culture, spirits can also come from a parallel universe and can fluctuate from that world into our material world. A nocturnal tormented spirit may be pleasant by day. It may also appear, perhaps, at your local Publix supermarket or some other ordinary location. Think twice before you tell off that cashier!!

Spiritual evil: Gullah people believe that illness comes from spiritual evil; that's why medicine alone cannot effect a cure. Black magic or folk magic is required.

Sprinkling powder: Used in gris-gris bags, sprinkled on a person or around a house for protection.

St. Helena Island: Home of the fascinating Gullah people, who were given land and freedom by the Union Army following the War Between the States. Their lyrical language, artistic tendencies, flavorful seafood dishes, and unique root-based history make it a lovely place to visit, but perhaps not at midnight in any garden of good and evil. Legend, lore and more abound. St. Helena was home to the infamous Dr. Buzzard, root doctor extraordinaire. Today, even this lovely coastal home to the famous Penn Center and charming Frogmore (and its Frogmore stew) faces problems with population growth, development, and such. But never fear, the dirt is deep here and will always be steeped in the root tradition.

St. Helena Parish: Part of a former English royal colony, located in Beaufort County, South Carolina. In spite of great encouragement/ coercion by early Episcopalian ministers to suppress native believes in voodoo, slaves (even after being baptized into a faith) continued their devotion and adherence to their native beliefs.

St. John's Eve: The most sacred of all voodoo celebrations.

Starbucks Spells?: Actually, any java will work. Coffee grounds can be read just as tea leaves. Coffee bean husk baths are used to uncross jinxes. Medically, coffee is a brain stimulant, diuretic, and laxative.

Stuffing (for voodoo dolls): Hair, Spanish moss, cotton, tobacco, wool, panty hose, and most anything else.

Things That Go Bump in the Night: Of all the explanations of voodoo in the Lowcountry, I found the preface to J. E. "High Sheriff of the Low Country" McTeer's book *Fifty Years as a Low Country Witch Doctor* the most accurate and moving. After all, he should know, having apprenticed as root conjurer with the infamous Dr. Buzzard. But more so, by having served as a young-to-old man as the arbiter of peace, justice, and understanding between the blacks and whites, the insiders and the outsiders, those who practice and believe in voodoo, and those who do not. So as not to plagiarize, I shall paraphrase his insightful concepts of the "weight of night" on people of the sea islands, who came from slavery and a lack of self-determination: While many of us sleep at peace in the night, others fear the dark. While some of us have access to solutions such as privilege or power, others may feel the need for other solutions. A quiet people, they kept such thoughts, feelings, and solutions close to their vests. If we could but peer through their haint blue-edged windows on a dark night, what might witness? Boo hags and such, potions and candles, altars to the black art of the Root, or ordinary activities? It is the intrigue that intrigues us, hey? As well as our appreciation of a culture long in the tooth; indeed, long may it live!

Thomas E. Ledbetter: Early Methodist minister who traveled the coastal Lowcountry attempting to purge embedded native devotion to roots and spells, considering such matters quite "unchristian." He was generally unsuccessful.

Ticket to Hide: A friend of mine served as a police officer in Port Royal, South Carolina. He recounted how he once stopped a driver and gave him a speeding ticket, not knowing that the man practiced serious root work. Not long after leaving the scene, the officer had a sudden, sharp, terrible, and quite debilitating pain in his side. "So bad," he said, "I had tears and felt the urgent need to go directly to an emergency room, the pain was so bad." Suffering through, the officer recovered. Later, he was called to the house of the sister of the man he had ticketed. When he got to her home, he found upside-down headless chickens hanging from her porch rails, as well as dried chicken heads adorning the posts. After he put two and two together, he realized that he'd been rooted. When he was later called to chase down that same speeding car, he wisely refused!

To throw for: Throwing down powders where a person is certain to walk through or over them.

Trabblin' spirits: Gullah term for the restless ghosts of those who were buried fast and never allowed a second burial.

Two-headed doctor: A root doctor or spiritual practitioner who is also a reader.

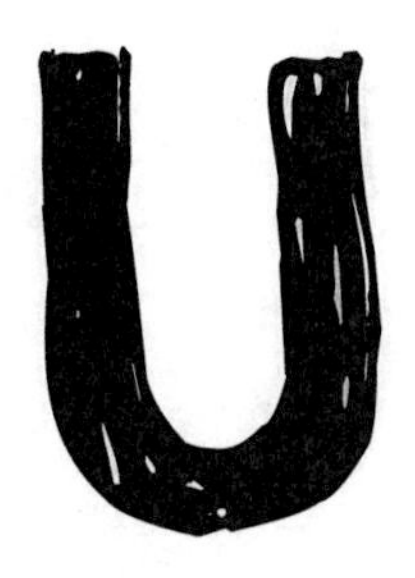

Ultimate Gullah: Visit ultimategullah.com to learn about and purchase Gullah products, such as sweetgrass baskets, art, spices, healing tonics, books, dolls and more; located in Conway, SC.

Unicorn root: Part of the lily family of plants, this root is also called Devil's Bit. Said to aid men in love affairs, an unbroken root must be used, usually dug in the wild. The root is claimed to enhance virility, especially when dressed daily with Stay With Me Oil. One can dream.

U.S. War Department: The generals must have been surprised to get a letter from Beaufort County, South Carolina sheriff Ed McTeer claiming voodoo was behind the illness of many would-be Gullah recruits headed to Ft. Jackson during World War II.

However, as the military continued to reject these men, suffering from heart palpitations (with no apparent good reason for them), the government took notice. Some men arrived critically ill; one died en route to the hospital.

Vending Voodoo: In Britain you can purchase voodoo dolls from mall vending machines.

Versatile Root Doctor

Don't need an impotence spell or a headache hex? Root doctors also seem to be well-versed in picking winning lottery numbers, controlling the role of dice, or the cutting of a deck of cards, as well as to affect the outcome of trials.

Voodoo: The word comes from the Dahomean word for spirit; also called conjuration, witchcraft, hoodoo or rootwork. A religious cult of African origin characterized by a belief in sorcery, fetishes and rituals in which participants communicate by trance with ancestors, saints, or animistic deities. [American Heritage Dictionary] Other names include ubia, black magic, 'the root' (a Gullah term).

Voodoo death: It has been proven that the expectation of dying, even from something like a hex, is quite powerful. Indeed, expectations powerfully affect a person's health. The physiology behind this may be related to the nerve to the heart causing the heart to gradually stop. So 'death by voodoo' can, and has, happened.

"I just made a voodoo doll of myself. Can someone take it to the gym?"

-Twitter post

Voodoo Dolls

Perhaps I'm the only person who thinks voodoo dolls are sort of cute and sweet, even adorable and needy-looking?! When I took Home Economics in high school, I would have liked sewing a lot more if we'd made voodoo dolls instead of aprons.

Voodoo dolls are basically hand-sewn effigies into which you insert straight pins to achieve some goal. That means a cheating husband or boyfriend might cry, "Ouch!" when you stabbed him hard THERE.

The use of voodoo dolls is common in many cultures, but, perhaps oddly, not especially in Haitian vodou or Louisiana voodoo. Such dolls originated in Europe as part of magical practices, although today they are considered more tied to African spirituality and folklore.

Dolls are commonly made of cloth or clay. (Clay from a crawdad hole is said to be best.) You can also make a cloth doll and stuff it with Spanish moss, herbs, straw, or cotton. Dress your voodoo dolls in corduroy and denim, making it look like the person you want to poke a pin into: blue thread for eyes; red yarn for hair, that kind of thing. While making your doll, create a ritual of chanting, burning incense, or some other ritual.

Poke your doll with colored pins in the appropriate areas: head=knowledge; heart=emotions; stomach=intuition. [See "Ouch!" to learn the meanings of each pin color.]

Voodoo dolls are not just for black magic; you can use them to do good, such as to snag a husband or wife, create success, or gain happiness.

Voodoo dolls, alternate names: Doll babies, baby dolls, dolls.

> I'm gonna make a voodoo doll of myself... and give it a massage.
>
> -Twitter

Voodoo in the courts: There have been many instances of trial evidence where parties claimed they'd been hexed or spelled or rooted. In the Lowcountry this is not a laughing matter. In one case, when a man was found innocent of charges, the loser in the case swore, "You won, but you won't live long enough to enjoy it!" He did not, killed in an accident just a short time later. In another case (perhaps of rooting gone awry), a man sentenced to die in the electric chair called for his witchdoctor. The doctor came, took the man's money, and attempted to help him via the dark arts. When the man eventually had his head shaved and electrodes stuck to his legs, he pleaded, "Doctor, don't you have any way to save me now?" The doctor advised: "Don't sit down, man, just don't sit down!"

Voodoo spirits: Loa, the twins, and the dead are considered the spiritual beings of voodoo.

Loa interact with people of the earth and are the spirits of the major forces in the universe—good, evil, health, and more. Loa are also contradictory: good and evil, happy and sad. The dead are the souls of your family members who have died, but not yet reclaimed. Ignore the dead at your peril; honor them and they may be helpful to you.

Voodoo Taboo

Common taboos, bad luck signs, or omens include:

- A clock that strikes 13 is a sign of a death to quickly come.
- A hooting owl is a bad omen.
- Don't bring a spade or hoe into your home.
- Don't start a project on a Friday; you will never finish it.
- If you head out and have to come back because you forgot something, be sure to make an X in the road before you turn around.

- It's bad luck to sleep with your hands clasped behind your head.
- It's bad luck to walk backwards.
- Never carry out ashes on Friday or between Christmas and New Year's Day.
- Never keep a crowing hen.
- Never lend someone matches.
- Never mend clothes while they are being worn.
- Never pay back borrowed salt.
- Never shake left hands, or you risk a curse on both shakers.
- Whatever you do, don't dream of chickens.

Voodoo terms: Other terms for voodoo include ubia, Santeria, the root, hoodoo.

Voodoo tools: Herbs, minerals, incense, anointing oils, sachet powders, bath crystals, candles, roots, personal possessions, parts of animals, such as a claw or feather, scripture.

Voodoo vaping: I have no idea what this is, but really…don't you wonder about all that eerie vape smoke?

Voodoo Village: Walter Eugene King left Detroit in 1970. He was determined to discover his African roots. Formerly a dancer with the Katherine Dunham Dance Company, King had traveled the world. He became fascinated with Haitian and African religious beliefs. He trekked to Nigeria, location of the former Yoruba Empire and Ifa religion. In 1959, he went to Cuba and became a Yoruba priest and changed his name. Later, King settled down at Sheldon, South Carolina, where he created Oyotunji Village, population 170. He proclaimed himself King Adefunmi (or Oba) and posted a sign at the village gate: YOU ARE NOW LEAVING THE UNITED STATES. His goal was to practice the ancient Yoruba faith of Ifa. Of course, locals were not too keen on the animal sacrifice, divination, and polygamy. Mostly, the apparent cult was gossiped about, but ignored. Eventually the area was referred to as "the voodoo village." For a fee, the king would, basically, conjure for you. When King died in 2005, he was said to have "gone up to the ceiling." It is possible that devotees still exist, waiting patiently to expand his faith far and wide. You can find the village off Safari Road, but it is private; however visitations are available on certain days.

Voodoo vocabulary: Perplexed by various spellings of all kinds of things, such as gris-gris, gree-gree, gui-gui, etc.? No worries, mate—such a long history of witchcraft, voodoo, vudou, voudon, hoodoo, as well as a variety of locations, have created a lack of consistency in spelling of terms that pretty much mean the same thing. As you might imagine, spellcheck was more like a 'spell' in proofing this book.

Vodou: A form of voodoo practiced in Haiti, New Orleans, and much of the Caribbean.

Voudoun: What voodoo is called in Western Africa; not the same as voudou (Haiti and New Orleans) or Santeria (Cuba).

Wateree Swamp, SC: Site of a frightening 'booger' encounter in 1936. It was called a "debilish critter" that could "run your pants off in the briars." When a man shot the booger six times, it turned into ash and cinders.

What's in a Name?: Why 'root' doctor? Well, witchdoctor, conjurer and sorcerer have negative connotations, so the term root doctor came into common usage. I guess it sounds much more organic and friendly!

When Gun Shoot: The Gullah Great Day of Jubilee, November 7, 1861, when a fleet of Union ships shot its way into Port Royal Sound and set troops ashore on the barrier islands.

Wiki-Huh?: Wikihow has some interesting comments on voodoo dolls (and I paraphrase):

To use classic torture techniques, use pins, needles, wire, rope, water, etc. Can you really waterboard a voodoo doll? And, "The powers of voodoo dolls have not been scientifically proven."

Witchcraft: Take the time to explore the history of witchcraft to better understand the beginnings of voodoo. The 'magical arts' of the Middle Ages coexisted with more traditional spiritual practices. The same could be said today. Warlocks, witches, werewolves, and others blossomed from the fear, mythology, hysteria, and misunderstandings that plagued those times. We witnessed such shenanigans in Salem, Massachusetts, with its colonial-era witch trials. There were reasonable origins for the occult; when we feel threatened, we seek aid where we can find it, believe in things that may help us. No wonder we feel hexed; no wonder we counter with spells. The less power you have, the more you cling to potential solutions of all kinds, using simple, easily obtainable tools—roots, herbs, candles, oils, incantations, fabric for effigies, and pins, to prove a point. And if you are unsure exactly how to pull off your plan, relieve your pain, gain success, wreak revenge (or even havoc), find love, and more, much more, you may seek out the person who specializes in such activities. Believe or not believe. Have YOU bought a lottery ticket lately? Ever read your horoscope? Had your palm read or fortune told? Witchcraft, voodoo, conjuring, etc. may or may not work, but they live. Indeed they do here in the Lowcountry!

Witchdoctors: What African medicine men are often erroneously called. In most cultures, witchdoctors seldom put hexes on people; they are more healers. A witch—well, that's a different story.

Wonder Books: Medieval works by Cornelius Agrippa, Albertus Magnus, and others, which were introduced to African Americans in the 19th century and have influenced hoodoo traditions.

X marks the spot: Perhaps you think voodoo is a bunch of hoodoo? Actually, many practitioners (see doctorbuzzard.com) include plenty of "fine print" to cover their voodooist butts, claiming quite explicitly that no spell can be guaranteed for a variety of reasons, including, but not limited to:

- A single spell may not be powerful enough if your situation is too deep-rooted or complex.
- A spell may not be enough; you may need to purchase products to enhance optimum results.
- You have excessive negative energy.
- You are unrealistic.
- It's just not meant to be: "the universe has other plans for you."

And now, you have been officially and thoroughly disclaimed.

Yarrow: Said to protect from wounds and make you brave. In Lowcountry lore, placing a packet of yarrow beneath your pillow will make you dream about the person you will marry.

Yoruba religion: Began in Africa, in Nigeria and the Republic of Benin. Yorubas were taken as slaves (just as the Gullah were) to America and Cuba. This religion practices animal sacrifice, polygamy, and divination.

Yucca: Yucca plant spikes can be used in voodoo dolls in lieu of pins.

Zombie: A corpse revived via voodoo to do whatever the conjurer demands; also spelled zombi.

Bibliography

There is a wealth of books on voodoo; often just reading the titles gives a glimpse into the breadth and depth of this vast subject. Examples: *Aunt Sally's Policy Players Dream Book; Voodoo Honey and Sugar Spells; Hoodoo Food! Throwing the Bones; Golden Secrets of Mystic Oils; Tea Cup Reading,* and more, many more. Perhaps none meets the magic of this title: *Albertus Magnus: Being the Approved, Verified, Sympathetic and Natural Egyptian Secrets: White and Black Art For Man and Beast, Revealing the Forbidden Knowledge and Mysteries of Ancient Philosophers* (on folk magic, AKA hoodoo/voodoo).

Africanisms in American Culture by Joseph Holloway

American Voudou: Journey into a Hidden World by Rod Davis

The Black Border: Gullah Stories of the Carolina Coast by Ambrose Gonzales

Blue Roots: African-American Folk Magic of the Gullah People by Roger Pinckney

"Boo Hags" by Chalmers S. Murray, **South Carolina Folktales: Stories of Animals and Supernatural Beings** compiled by Workers of the Writer's Program of the Work Projects Administration, 1941

Charms, Spells and Formulas for the Making and Use of Gris-Gris, Herb Candles, Doll Magick, Incenses, Oils and Powders—To Gain Love, Protection, Prosperity, Luck, and Prophetic Dreams by Ray T. Malbrough

Coffin Point: The Strange Cases of Ed McTeer, WitchDoctor Sheriff by Baynard Woods

Doctor to the Dead: Grotesque Legends and Folk Tales of Old Charleston by John Bennett

Fifty Years as a Low Country Witch Doctor by J.E. McTeer

Folk Beliefs of the Southern Negro by Newbell Niles Puckett and Patterson Smith

The Golden Bough: A Study of Magic and Religion by Sir James George Frazer

The Gullah Mailman by Pierre McGowan

Haitian Vodou: An Introduction to Haiti's Indigenous Spiritual Tradition by Mambo Chita Tann

The Half-Pint Flask by DuBose Heyward
A short story by Charleston author DuBose Heyward. In this tale, a plateye spirit of a former lover torments a man almost to commit suicide. In real life, people have been known to actually kill themselves.

The Handbook of Yoruba Religious Concepts by Baba Ifa Karade

Hoodoo and Conjure Quarterly, Denise Alvarado, Editor

Hoodoo, Conjurations, Witchcraft, Rootwork, Volumes I and II by Harry M. Hyatt

Hoodoo Herb and Root Magic: A Materia Magica of African-American Conjure by Catherine Yronwode, former staff editor for *Organic Gardening Magazine*; at 224 pages, 500 herbs, roots, minerals, and rare zoological curios, plus 750 spells, this book is a useful compendium of conjuring!

Hoodoo Medicine: Gullah Herbal Remedies by Faith Mitchell

Lowcountry Conjuring Tales... *"The Apothecary's Folly," "The Boo Hag Bride," "Doctor to the Dead," "Haints in the Keyhole House," "Hound of Goshen," "Why You Shouldn't Mess With Voodoo"*

Lowcountry Voodoo: Beginner's Guide to Tales, Spells and Boo Hags by Terrance Zepke and Michael Swing

Midnight in the Garden of Good and Evil by John Berendt
The movie by the same name was filmed in Savannah and directed by Clint Eastwood; starring Kevin Spacey, it's definitely worth viewing for the Bonaventure voodoo scene.

The Mind Game: Witchdoctors and Psychiatrists by E. Fuller Torrey

Rootwork: Psychosocial Aspects of Malign Magical Illness Beliefs in a South Carolina Sea Island Community by Kathryn Wilson Heyer; Dissertation, Department of Sociology, University of Connecticut, 1981

The Serpent and the Rainbow: A Harvard Scientist's Astonishing Journey into the Secret Societies of Haitian Voodoo, Zombis, and Magic by Wade Davis

Sherlock Holmes Investigates. The Case of Lady Chatterley's Voodoo Dolls by Philip van Wulven
This story has nothing to do with the Lowcountry. I include it here as more of a "Who knew?" than a hoodoo.

Tales of Edisto by Nell Graydon

Voodoo and Hoodoo: The Craft as Revealed by Traditional Practitioners by Jim Haskins

Voodoo, Devils, and the New Invisible World by Daniel Cohen

The Voodoo Doll Spellbook: A Compendium of Ancient and Contemporary Spells and Rituals by Denise Alvarado

The Voodoo Hoodoo Spellbook by Denise Alvarado and Doktor Snake
A review said, "No magical workspace is complete without it!" Gee, I wish I had a magical workspace.

Voodoo Queen: The Spirited Lives of Marie Laveau by Martha Ward

The Voodoo Times: Just a random sampling of real headlines in Lowcountry media—"Body Unearthed, Head Cut Off in Voodoo Ritual"…"Voodoo Alive and Well in S. C. Lowcountry"…"Marine Thankful to be Free of Evil"…"Dr. Bug, Dr. Buzzard and the U.S.A."…"Former Beaufort Sheriff Known as Low Country Witch Doctor"…"Former Sheriff Fights Witchcraft with White Magic"… "Witchcraft Lives."

Resources

African American Heritage Trails: Two separate trails through the South Carolina Lowcountry feature museums, galleries, dining and more that showcase the cultural heritage. The African American Coastal Trail starts at McClellanville and ends just past Edisto Island. Highlights include plantations such as Boone Hall and Hampton, Forts Moultrie and Sumter, churches, the Old Slave Mart Museum, and more. The Folkways and Communities Trail includes North Charleston, Walterboro, the South Carolina Artisans Center, cemeteries, Middleton Place, Magnolia Plantation and Gardens, Drayton Hall, Charles Towne Landing, and other sites.

Avery Research Center for African American History and Culture: Research, exhibits and tours. College of Charleston, 125 Bull Street.

Charleston County Public Library: A great place to research all things Lowcountry, Gullah, and voodoo.

Gullah Flea Market: 103 William Hilton Parkway, Hilton Head Island, SC.

Gullah/Geechee Cultural Heritage Corridor: Stretches from Wilmington, NC to Jacksonville, FL. In 2004, the National Trust for Historic Preservation named the Gullah/Geechee coast as one of America's most endangered historic places. With native people dying out and the young people moving away, the culture and land are also under negative impact through higher taxes due to development creating rising property values. Nonetheless, many of the people continue to live in the old ways and fish, farm, sell handmade craft items such as sweetgrass baskets, or work at the many resorts in the Hilton Head Island and other resort areas.

Gullah O'oman Shop and Museum: Learn about the Gullah traditions and language. Purchase handmade quilts, clothing, sweetgrass baskets, toys, and more. Pawleys Island, SC.

Penn Center and York W. Bailey Museum: Highlights the Gullah history and culture;

extensive collection of papers, documents and recordings. National Historic Landmark since 1974. Originally a school for freed slaves; later a center of reform. Martin Luther King, Jr. planned his March on Washington here. Today the museum preserves Sea Island and Lowcountry African American heritage.

Acknowledgements

Alan Wright for his ineluctable enthusiasm for Lowcountry voodoo!

Phoenix Douglas, for fascinating stories told in her inimitable Lowcountry Gullah patois.

Caregiver extraordinaire Laverne Doe, for sharing her boo hag story and grandma tales.

Caregiver Shalaya Robertson for examples of "being rooted."

Reverend Ralph Bailey for his stories from the Lowcountry.

Baynard Woods, for writing *Coffin Point: The Strange Cases of Ed McTeer, WitchDoctor Sheriff*, and stirring my interest and making me gasp!

John Berendt for *Midnight in the Garden of Good and Evil*, making me a fan of Jim Williams, and showcasing some of Savannah and the Lowcountry intrigue.

Joyce Sipple, for cluing me in to the cemetery on our own property, as well as her enthusiasm for my project and recommending a voodoo museum to visit.

Mark May for an extraordinary story shared in this book.

Susan Van Denhende, for making my books look good, the art, and her youthful enthusiasm for all subjects.

My Chapter III Palmetto Bluff book club buddies: We read! We read!

Janice Baker, John Hanson, Jon McKenna, Chrisa Gamez, Candy Persons, Vivian Bernstein, and all at Gallopade for making me look and sound good all the time. This certainly includes Michael Longmeyer and Michele Yother, who put up with my curious interests.

Thanks to magical photographer Nancy McGregor for the fun photo shoot in the graveyard and the gorgeous prints.

My husband, Bob Longmeyer, for always supporting my interests, and always being interesting.

My new rescue pup, Coconut, for keeping me company at night while I wrote; not so much for growling at shadows…*or were they?*

About the Author

Carole Marsh Longmeyer is an author and publisher who now lives on the bluffs of the May River in the Lowcountry of South Carolina. She has spent most of her career educating, entertaining and intriguing young readers with her 100 Carole Marsh Mysteries set in real locales around the nation and the world. "This," she says, "is my new voodoo hat, although I do not exactly know what that means—yet!"

About the Designer and Illustrator

Susan Van Denhende is an illustrator and book designer who earned her BFA in Sequential Art from the Savannah College of Art and Design. She now lives in the vast, sprawling city that is Jacksonville, Florida. She has spent most of her life reading and loves that her art allows her to work with books—especially when she gets free copies of the books she works on. You can find her work at auroradoesart.com.